Make the Most of Your Caravan

Rob McCabe

Rob McCabe is one of the UK's most experienced caravanning journalists. In a long career working on a wide variety of newspapers and magazines, including *The Sunday Post*, *Motor Cycle News*, *Take A Break* and *What Car?* he has edited two caravan magazines – *Practical Caravan* and *Caravan* – and contributed to several others. He is a regular contributor of caravan tests to *The Caravan Club Magazine*, the UK's largest-circulation caravanning title, and writes a monthly caravanning column that appears in several regional daily and weekly newspapers, and online.

Rob lives in Cambridgeshire with his wife Rachel and two sons, Angus and Sol.

Teach® Yourself

Make the Most of Your Caravan

Rob McCabe

First published in Great Britain in 2007 by Hodder Education. An Hachette UK company.

First published in US in 2007 by The McGraw-Hill Companies, Inc.

This edition published 2014

Previously published as *Teach Yourself Caravanning*

British Library Cataloguing in Publication Data: a catalogue record for this title is available from the British Library.

Library of Congress Catalog Card Number: on file.

10 9

Cover image © Jim Vecchi / Alamy

Typeset by Cenveo® Publisher Services.

Printed and bound in Great Britain by Clays Ltd, Elcograf S.p.A.

Hodder & Stoughton policy is to use papers that are natural, renewable and recyclable products and made from wood grown in sustainable forests. The logging and manufacturing processes are expected to conform to the environmental regulations of the country of origin.

Hodder & Stoughton Ltd

338 Euston Road

London NW1 3BH

www.hodder.co.uk

Contents

Foreword by Dame Margaret Beckett, DBE, MP

I am very pleased to see that caravanning remains as popular today as when I started out. This comprehensive guide provides a wealth of useful information for the next generation of caravan fans. I hope it will inspire and give confidence to anyone thinking about trying a caravan holiday for the first time. But even for someone like me, a caravan enthusiast for many years, there are plenty of useful tips and new ideas.

My own passion for caravan holidays has been occasionally commented on by the media! It is certainly something of which I am proud. But I am not the only fan. There has been a recent trend towards this leisure pursuit among a number of household names. Certainly, Jamie Oliver and his camper van are pretty famous! Not only is it highly enjoyable, but it is fast becoming a lifestyle choice.

The types of caravans available today are mind-boggling, ranging from the truly state of the art with all the mod cons for pop stars on tour, to the more functional family caravan. Caravanning can be as simple or as luxurious as you choose. It is all down to personal preference. My own caravanning experience is probably not dissimilar to that of many families across the country who also share this hobby.

It best suits those who enjoy the freedom of being able to take to the open road and end up in any number of interesting and beautiful places. My husband and I have enjoyed many summer holidays on the continent, and many people say that their most memorable trips have been the journeys made on the spur of the moment. Travelling in this way allows real spontaneity. You can decide at the last minute to go on a break without having to worry about plane or train tickets or finding a suitable hotel.

Some people think that going on a caravan holiday is a slightly more upscale version of camping. Let me assure you, it is much better than that. You know that you will have your creature comforts wherever you are. I never have to pack light and I can put the kettle on in any location. My caravan has become my home away from home.

And last but not least, when it comes to the environment, the caravan is a relatively environmentally friendly way to take your holiday; it gives off only a fraction of the greenhouse gas emissions compared to travelling by air. That's as good a motivation as any to make caravanning a habit for life.

Whatever your inspiration for taking up caravanning, I hope that readers will find this guide a useful introduction. And I hope that you will enjoy your own 'mobile holidays' as much as I have over the years.

Margaret Beckett

Introduction

I can (just about ...) remember the first time I took a caravan away on my own. It was only a one-night stay and there was a bit of headscratching involved, a bit of trial and error. But I had a great time and I came away much the wiser. There is, after all, no substitute for experience.

And I've used that experience – built up over many years in caravanning journalism – to compile this book, *Make the Most of Your Caravan*. While writing it, I never once lost sight of the fact that I, too, had once been a raw novice. I can still remember the things I wish I had known when I was trial-and-erroring my way through those earliest trips away. I've made sure that these have all been addressed within these pages.

What's the best way to describe caravanning? That's a very good question to be starting out with. There are more than half a million caravanners in the UK alone; and if you were to ask each of them, you'd get a wide variety of answers – some of which may include the reasons that have sparked your own interest.

For many caravanners, 'interest' underplays it somewhat; 'passion' would more accurately describe the relationship that they have with their caravans and with caravanning in general. What fires that passion, then?

▶ For some, it's the love of the caravan itself; the pride of ownership that comes with using, maintaining and improving a vehicle that makes them feel better about it every time they go away in it.

▶ There's another thing that enthuses people, too – the ability to be up and off wherever, and whenever, they feel like it. A lot of those half-million caravanners will use the same word when asked that opening question: freedom.

▶ A caravan is arguably the best way of experiencing the countryside, due to the incredible spread of caravan sites, large and small, throughout the entire United Kingdom and the European mainland. Some idyllic, tucked-away corners of the countryside are accessible only to the landowner – and caravanners. You'll find out about these special places in this book.

▶ Caravanners quickly come to love the fact that, when they reach their destination, they're free of worry about what their holiday accommodation will look (or smell …) like when they throw open the door. It's the same every time; it's the accommodation they chose when they bought the caravan; it's the accommodation that will feel more and more like home the more they use it.

▶ Every caravan has a payload, i.e. a weight allowance for personal belongings, that gives couples or families the wherewithal to take far more luggage than any other kind of holiday could accommodate. Think you may want to go cycling when you get there? Your caravan will accommodate the bikes. And the helmets. And the rucksacks. And a weekend's worth of beer and wine. And all your food. And your clothes. And your bedding. And the TV. No need for the kitchen sink – there's one built in.

▶ For a lot of people, all the above happily apply – but the main factor is that they can go caravanning reasonably cheaply. Although it has long since ceased to be the case that low cost is the main reason why most people take up caravanning, it is still possible to have a great time on a tight budget. Families who may not otherwise have been able to contemplate a summer holiday can go off and see new places, meet new people and come home thrilled by the experience and positively itching to get away in the caravan again.

Yes, you should be warned before you go any further that caravanning is like that: it's rare, if not unheard of, for people to give caravanning a go and come away positively underwhelmed by the experience.

However, there's no point in trying to pretend that ownership of a caravan is a bed of sweet-smelling roses all the time. Hopefully, the advice, the suggestions and the ideas contained in this book will make sure those thorny issues that do exist are minimized or eliminated.

So, what are the potential problems that may lie in wait?

▶ A caravan obviously has to be kept somewhere when not in use. If you can't keep it at home, you'll need to find a suitable storage location – and that can be expensive. Maybe there isn't a good storage site within reasonable distance of home, in which case it can be inconvenient just getting to and from your caravan.

▶ A caravan is a fairly complex vehicle with mechanical moving parts, as well as a plethora of gas- and electricity-powered appliances on board. Like all machines, it can go wrong – and so a good relationship with your dealer is crucial. So, too, is a regime of basic but essential maintenance.

▶ Although many sites are fantastically cheap, a caravanning holiday can be on the expensive side – especially when you factor in the cost of buying, maintaining and storing the caravan on top of site fees and travelling expenses.

▶ There are so many different layouts of caravan available, the choice can be bewildering. Getting this particular bit wrong can spoil your enjoyment of the vehicle.

▶ You may find that the car you own, and with which you are otherwise perfectly happy, isn't physically capable of towing the type of caravan you would really like.

▶ Caravans are targeted by thieves, so you must budget for a range of good anti-theft devices and take out the appropriate insurance cover.

WHY YOU NEED THIS BOOK

There's a lot to consider even before you buy your first caravan, so in this book you'll find lots of detailed information about what model will suit you best, what kind of equipment you can expect to find on board and where to buy one. Should you buy new or used? Dealer or private sale? Basic or fully featured? All these questions are addressed.

After you take delivery of your new caravan, there's a lot of know-how to take on board; know-how that, unless you have a bit of guidance, can take years of experience to accrue.

The aim of this book is to get you up and running with your caravan – and caravanning – as quickly as possible: making sure you have a car that will tow your caravan safely; knowing how to set the caravan up when you arrive on site for the first time; having some idea of the best places to take your caravan, whether at home or abroad; making sure your caravan is safely and securely loaded; how to protect it from theft; using it in the winter … and much more.

Throughout the book, you'll find lots of 'Key point' and 'Remember this' boxes, covering everything to do with the world of caravanning. They're invaluable nuggets of information, some of which have been passed on to me by caravanners with hundreds of years of experience between them.

And for those at the other end of the experience spectrum, I hope you enjoy reading this book almost as much as you enjoy the adventure of choosing – and using – your first caravan.

Rob McCabe
April 2014

1

Buying your first caravan

In this chapter, you will learn:

▶ *why a cheap caravan makes sense as a great first buy*

▶ *the anatomy of a caravan – what kind of equipment you can expect to find and how all the on-board systems work*

▶ *the pros and cons of buying new or second-hand.*

Jim and Margaret Forrester have been caravanning for 17 years. They've earned the right to introduce this first chapter because the way they went about cutting their caravanning teeth all those years ago is a shining example of the right way to go about it.

The Forresters had talked about acquiring a caravan as a means of having summer holidays and weekends away with their two (then very young) children. However, they were unsure if caravanning really would be for them and, as such, didn't want to commit to a multi-thousand-pound transaction.

Jim suggested they track down a cheap, older caravan from the local paper small ads and give it a try. A few weeks later, he found one: sure, it was a bit rough around the edges, but it was clean and dry, and easy to tow. He paid the seller the £280 asking price and brought it home.

The Forresters loved their trips away in the old caravan, even though on-board facilities could best be described as rudimentary and the accommodation was somewhat cramped. They'd seen enough: if they could have a whale of a time in such a small, basic caravan, imagine how they'd get on in a larger, more up-to-date model with all the mod cons.

They took the plunge, treated themselves to a new caravan and never looked back – although, with their kids now grown up, they enjoy caravanning on their own.

It was a faultless strategy. If Jim and Margaret had found that the caravanning lifestyle just wasn't working out as they'd hoped it would, they'd have shrugged their shoulders, sold the old caravan – almost certainly recouping their initial investment in the process – and gone and booked an apartment in Magaluf or Benidorm. Had they splashed out on a £10,000 family caravan from a local dealer, they'd have had to cut their losses and would have been quite substantially out of pocket.

It was a superbly logical thing to do, even if they did perhaps take things to extremes by buying such a bargain-basement, elderly model. They could have spent just a few hundred pounds more and benefited from a bit more luxury and extra living space.

While you need to be realistic about what you're buying at the cheap end of the market – you're not looking for perfection – you should still be looking to buy a vehicle that is, above all, safe for the road and safe to live in.

Key point

Not only does buying an older, low-cost caravan limit your initial outlay, you're also highly likely to get at least what you paid for it when you resell, because decent-quality, cheap caravans rarely depreciate, such is the ongoing demand.

If you're willing to spend a day thoroughly cleaning the inside and outside of a scruffy old caravan, you may even double its value.

Remember this

In your hunt for a low-cost starter caravan, you may face competition from hill farmers who want to install a shelter in one of the more remote corners of their land...

What's in a caravan?

That's a real 'how long is a piece of string?' question. However, the majority of tourers have some shared features. ('Tourer' is just another name for the 'touring caravan', which you'll see mentioned throughout the book.)

There's only one common link to every caravan, though: they all consist of a rolling chassis with either one or two axles, on to which is added a floor and the enveloping bodywork – overwhelmingly consisting of separate sidewalls, front and rear panels and a roof. Some models, notably the diminutive Polish-built caravans marketed in the UK as 'Freedom', have one-piece moulded bodies. In recent years, mainstream UK manufacturers including Bailey, the Explorer Group and the Swift Group have embraced new construction methods that are claimed to offer increased strength and rigidity at the same time as reducing greatly the risk of water ingress.

The range of layouts, furniture and equipment you'll find in caravans varies enormously.

THE BASICS

If you are looking for what basically amounts to a tent with walls, the only requirements are for:

▶ enough beds to accommodate everyone

▶ somewhere to sit in the evening

▶ a 12-volt leisure battery to power some lights

▶ a gas supply to operate a couple of rings on a hob

▶ a few cupboards to store things in

▶ a cold-water system for teeth-brushing

▶ maybe a toilet compartment, even if you need to bring your own portable loo.

Almost every caravan, no matter how cheap, should fulfil these less-than-exacting demands.

THE NEXT STEP UP

What if you'd like just a few more creature comforts?

▶ You may want a mains electric system that connects to the site supply by means of a cable. This allows you to use appliances such as a TV, kettle, CD player, charger for mobile phone/tablet or even a low-wattage microwave.

▶ If you're using the caravan outside the summer months, you'll certainly need a heater to stop the caravan feeling like a cold store, especially at night.

▶ Maybe you'd like a water heater so you can do the odd bit of washing-up or to freshen up if the weather's just too awful to contemplate a walk to the washing-up room or the shower block.

▶ If you want to do more than warm up some soup, you'll need more gas rings, and a grill for toast.

▶ A fridge is nigh-on indispensable for a stay of more than a night or two.

▶ It would be nice to have a shower attachment in the washroom, even if only to rinse off sandy feet after a day on the beach.

Once again, a high percentage of second-hand caravans – and nearly every new one these days – will include all the above, which pretty much takes care of all the essentials. The majority of more recent caravans will have an oven (well worth having), a roof-mounted TV aerial, blinds and flyscreens on most, if not all, windows, and a stabilizer built into the hitch (the part that attaches to the towball on the towing vehicle). Most newer caravans above entry-level status will have a built-in microwave.

Remember this

If you feel that you're somehow missing out because your caravan doesn't have a microwave, you can always buy a cheap one and keep it for caravan use. There are low-wattage models, but a normal domestic one will work perfectly well as long as you don't use the hairdryer, kettle and electric heater at the same time. Many caravans will have an overhead locker in the kitchen area big enough to accommodate one; an electrician can easily fit a discreet additional mains socket.

As you look around the forecourts or trawl through the classified ads, you'll also come across fitted stereo radio/CD players (many of which have connectivity for iPods and other portable music players), roof-mounted electric extractor fans, tilt-and-slide sunroofs (now quite common on newer models), a pair of mains-powered lights to complement the usual 12-volt lighting system, electronic security alarms and even air-conditioning.

If you're buying second-hand, you stand to benefit from the equipment the previous owner has bought for the caravan. Such essentials as a 12-volt leisure battery, a 25-metre mains hook-up lead, a spare wheel and carriers for both fresh and waste water may be included in the sale. If not, you'll need to buy them. If you're lucky, an awning (of which more in Chapter 2) will be included as well.

If you're treating yourself to a brand-new caravan, the mains lead will be included, but check about everything else – every dealer's 'on the road' package is different. It's especially a shame that not every caravan is sold with a spare wheel and jack as standard; it's like asking you to pay extra for the key to unlock the door.

THE CARAVAN'S STRUCTURE

When pitched, a caravan rests on four metal feet – corner steadies – that are attached to the chassis and which wind all the way up when not in use. Not everywhere you want to camp will have perfectly level ground, of course – but we'll be looking at how you overcome that in Chapter 7.

When the steadies are up, the caravan is supported by the so-called jockey wheel, which sits at the front of the chassis – a part known as the A-frame. The telescopic leg attached to the jockey wheel allows a wide range of vertical adjustment via the winder, enabling easy attachment to the towing vehicle, and front-to-back levelling of the caravan on site.

Right alongside the jockey wheel lives the handbrake and the electrical leads that plug into the appropriate sockets next to the towball on the towcar. Caravans made from 2008-onwards will have just a single 13-pin electrical socket, so adhering to European Union legislation. Don't worry if your car and caravan electrical sockets are a mismatch – you can buy the necessary adaptor for just a few pounds.

In the majority of cases, the caravan's sides consist of an aluminium skin on the outside, the interior wall covering on the inside and a layer of insulation in between. The same insulating material is used on the floor, sandwiched between two thin layers of wood.

The roof is usually a covering of aluminium skin, although some are made of GRP (glassfibre-reinforced plastic). The front and rear panels may also be GRP or aluminium, but plastic is very common.

Figure 1.1 A caravan is a complex vehicle with moving mechanical parts and its own plumbing, gas and electrical systems. There's plenty to learn!

How do all the systems work?

It's really straightforward to set up a caravan to operate as your home from home when you've arrived on site and pitched it. Again, this is something we'll look at in more detail in Chapter 7, but there's not much more to it than this whistle-stop summary.

ELECTRICITY AND GAS

If you're connecting to the site's mains electricity supply, do that first. On an interior wall of the caravan, you may see a rocker switch that shifts the 12-volt operation from the car you've been towing with to the caravan – flick that switch.

Chances are your LPG (liquefied petroleum gas) cylinder or cylinders will be in the exterior locker at the front, under the front window (on some, they're in a locker on the side wall). If your caravan was made before 1 September 2003, each gas bottle will have its own regulator. Turn on the one with the regulator connected – there will always be an arrow on the knob on top of the cylinder that allows you to check and double-check whether or not your gas is turned on. More recent models will also have a plastic lever that needs to be flicked on (i.e. parallel with the gas pipe it's connected to). On caravans built from 1 September 2003 onwards, the regulator is attached to the wall of the gas locker itself. This runs at a pressure that accommodates both propane and butane – there's no need to have a separate regulator for both, as with models predating 1 September 2003.

That's it – you now have power to make all the on-board systems work.

▶ All caravan fridges are clever. They can work either off gas if you're not connected to the site electricity supply or from the car's 12-volt battery when on the move. But for the purposes of this illustration you are connected up – so make sure that the fridge is switched appropriately.

▶ The caravan will probably have a transformer/battery charger that switches the power from 12-volt (battery) to mains electricity and also keeps the leisure battery fully charged while you're connected to the mains. Only the most basic models don't have this handy device fitted as standard, although you can usually pay a bit more to have your supplying dealer add one before you take delivery.

▶ If the site is so basic that there's no mains hook-up available, the caravan's lighting will be provided by the on-board 12-volt leisure battery. Fridge, cooker, heater and water heater will run on gas.

▶ Each gas appliance (cooker, fridge, heater and water heater) is served by its own on–off tap. They'll probably all be grouped together inside a floor-level cupboard; make sure they're turned to the 'on' position.

WATER

In most cases, when you fill your fresh-water container, you park it next to the water-pump socket on the caravan's exterior sidewall.

▶ Plug in the appropriate end of the submersible water pump to said socket, place the other end in the water container and go inside to turn the water-pump switch to 'on'.

▶ When you turn the tap at the kitchen sink and/or wash-hand basin or turn the shower on, the pump will switch itself on, draw water in from the container via the submersible and carry it around the caravan's network of fresh-water hoses. Switching the pump on also draws water into the hot water tank.

▶ Some caravans have an internal water tank that fills itself from the external container via a 12-volt pump – a neat idea if you intend to use the caravan throughout the winter because it minimizes the risk of your water supply freezing up.

▶ With your water connected, you can now turn on the water heater. On most caravans, you can run this on gas or electric or, if you're in a real hurry for hot water, both. Cheaper caravans may have a mains-electric-only water heater, or even just a cold-water-only supply.

▶ When you run the taps (or drain some water from a pan), the water disappears down the plug hole and into the caravan's waste-water pipes. They will converge on either one or two – or, occasionally, three – waste-water outlets at the side or rear of the caravan, to which you should attach a short length of ribbed waste hose that, in turn, is placed in the neck of a waste-water container.

TOILETS

Most caravan washrooms have a highly civilized cassette toilet, into which you pour the appropriate chemical solution to make life that bit more civilized still. Use a kettle or jug to fill up the separate flushing header tank.

Every time you use the toilet, the contents of the toilet bowl are flushed into the cassette tank. When nearly full, you empty the cassette tank at the dedicated chemical disposal point. It's a fundamental facility offered by every site, no matter how basic or remote.

New v. second-hand – the pros and cons

Who doesn't like being the first owner of anything? Whether it's a gleaming bicycle wheeled straight from the shop or a beautifully presented book, the spine delightfully stiff and the pages pristine, there's an immense amount of satisfaction to be had from owning something so new.

A caravan is no different. In fact, being the moving, component-laden vehicle it is, the feeling is, if anything, more pronounced.

NEW IS GREAT, BECAUSE ...

... you're happy and secure in the knowledge that no one else has slept on that bed, or spattered goose fat all over the oven, or neglected to have the brakes checked. You have the comfort zone of a full manufacturer's warranty ... and this year's soft furnishing colour scheme is fresh and modern.

ON THE OTHER HAND...

... it costs. Most new caravans are expensive to buy in the first place and, being the first owner, you also take the biggest hit when it comes to depreciation – i.e. the amount your caravan drops in value from the moment it becomes registered in your name. You may be able to find a three- or four-year-old model that looks brand-new and will save you thousands of pounds. Let's assume for the moment that this argument holds more sway and that you've decided to buy used.

Buying second-hand

If you buy a used caravan, you save money, of course – and we've considered already how you might benefit from accessories and upgrades carried out by (or on behalf of) the previous owner as part of the deal.

Depending on what layout you're looking for – an absolutely critical consideration, which gets its very own chapter in this book – you may even stand a better chance of finding your ideal caravan second-hand, especially if you don't want to wait too long to get your hands on it. When buying new, it's not always as straightforward as walking into a dealer's showroom, pointing to a model from the newly released brochure and proclaiming: 'I'd like that one, please.' It could be that the next batch isn't even due on the production line for weeks or, depending on the time of year, it could be sold out.

WHERE TO BUY

When you start doing the rounds of caravans on your shortlist, always take someone with you, especially if he or she has a caravanning background. But where should you do the rounds? Should you buy from a dealer or go private? As with a used car, it's cheaper to buy privately: the dealer has to make his profit, after all. The trade-off is a lack of comeback.

▶ If you buy from a private seller and the caravan turns out to be a rogue, that's an awkward situation to be in. You're pretty much stuck with it.

▶ If you encounter a problem having bought from a reputable dealer, though, you know where to take the caravan back to. Dealers often offer warranties with their used caravans, even if they are valid for only a few weeks or months. That's absolutely fine – it's certainly enough time for you to identify any inherent faults. Indeed, unless the caravan in question is in the bargain-basement 'look, just get this thing off my forecourt' category, you should be wary if it's being offered for sale without any sort of warranty at all.

Establishing a good relationship with a caravan dealership you like and trust is highly desirable, whether you've bought new or used.

If you're lucky, your caravan will behave itself and not give you any cause to beat a path back to the dealer. But they are machines and they do go wrong; when they do, it's reassuring to know you're being looked after.

And, like it or not, you'll probably find yourself higher up the waiting list when booking a service if you bought the caravan from the dealer in question.

However much you've set aside to buy your caravan, don't forget to add the cost of insurance, any essential equipment that's not included in the transaction and, if the vehicle hasn't had one recently, a full service.

Remember this

One useful tool when searching for a caravan (or anything else) on eBay is the ability to place the listings in order of distance from your home postcode. So, if you don't want to travel more than about 20 miles to have a look at any that attract your interest, you can just disregard the ones that fall outside your search area.

Key point

Even though you may choose to decide that getting a service isn't a priority, do have the gas system on a second-hand caravan checked by a suitably qualified technician. If you get to the end of this book and feel you can only take one piece of advice, make it this one.

Consider this example of a 'caravan for sale' private classified ad:

> Light but regular use; serviced annually (all invoices kept);
> shower never even turned on; owned since new by non-
> smoking dog haters. Full awning included.

It's a convoluted example, of course, but it ticks virtually all the right boxes. Let's dissect it to find out why.

▶ 'Light but regular use'

This is important because it means the caravan hasn't been laid up for long periods at a time, and therefore that doors and windows have been opened frequently.

That, in turn, means it's less likely to be suffering from damp – which you'll sometimes hear described as 'water ingress'. But why use two words when one will do? It's damp – and it's to be avoided at all costs. Although an isolated patch of rotten wood can be cut out and replaced, the very fact that it's there at all begs other questions that are probably better asked rhetorically after you've walked away and gone to find another caravan to look at.

You may be able to smell damp when you walk in the door, but it may not be as obvious as the pongs caused by dogs and cigarette smoke. Make sure you inspect every nook, cranny and crevice, looking for the tell-tale patches of discoloration on walls or ceiling, or unsightly black, mouldy spots.

It may be helpful to buy, hire or borrow a damp meter, but only if you know how to collate the information it gives you: a certain amount of moisture is to be expected in a perfectly healthy caravan. Make sure it's a dry day when you use it.

Your fine-toothed-comb search for damp also gives you the opportunity to open every single door, cupboard, drawer and bed base lid – how else will you know if they're all in one piece, and that they open and close as they should?

What caused the patch of dampness to appear – is it symptomatic of a vehicle that's been less than well cared for? Are there other hidden patches just waiting to make their presence known minutes after you've bought the caravan?

You shouldn't be misled into thinking that it's only older caravans that suffer from damp. Water may have seeped in through inadequate sealing of body panels at the factory – and there have been some horrendous cases of rot on caravans under five years old because of this.

▶ 'Serviced annually (all invoices kept)'

Not only can you be assured that all the on-board systems will be in tip-top condition, you will also encounter a caravan where all the corner steadies move effortlessly and the jockey wheel winds with silent efficiency. The paperwork proves to you that the brakes have been checked and that the tyres are in guaranteed good condition.

The fact that the owner has been so conscientious is also very likely to be reflected in the way he or she has looked after it: the toilet and cooker are probably spotless, and there's a good chance there won't be a speck of dust or a smear anywhere.

▶ 'Shower never even turned on'

This is good news because another cause of damp is over-liberal use of the shower; many of them aren't sufficiently isolated to keep water and condensation from doing their worst. In more recent years, some manufacturers have offered sealed shower cubicles, which are a boon both for those seeking to do their fair share of douching on board and for those looking to buy a watertight second-hand caravan.

▶ 'Owned since new'

If everything works and everything looks clean, take that as a sign of a caravan that has been cared for conscientiously throughout its life. A vehicle that's been owned from day one by a real caravanning enthusiast is probably a wise investment, in that caring for the caravan itself will have been as much of a passion for the owner as going away on holiday in it. There's a good chance the owner has struck up a good working relationship with the supplying dealer, who will be familiar with the caravan – you should make every effort to continue that relationship.

▶ 'Non-smoking dog hater'

First impressions count: take account of your first, split-second impression as you open the door and walk in. A caravan that smells strongly of stale cigarette smoke or dog is truly off-putting. Cigarette smoke also discolours the walls and ceiling. There's also the possibility that the upholstery or work surface will be damaged by a cigarette burn somewhere.

▶ 'Full awning included'

Pleasingly for those shopping on the used marketplace, this is actually quite common. The seller may not be replacing the caravan (in which case there's a good chance you'll get awning, water containers, cutlery, clothes pegs – the lot), or may be buying another caravan with completely different awning measurements. Getting an awning in good condition at a stroke does away with having to buy what, for most caravanners, is the most expensive item after the caravan itself.

YOUR PRE-PURCHASE CHECKLIST

The seller (or selling dealer) may strike you as being as honest and trustworthy as they come. However, don't let that stop you from asking them to turn on and demonstrate every single switch and appliance – and you should still give the caravan a thorough examination so that you're as satisfied as you can be that you're on to a good thing.

- ▶ As you walk around the caravan, watch out for a slightly spongy feeling underfoot. This is most likely to be caused by delamination, where the chemical bond between two panels has become separated. It's usually repairable, but can be expensive. My advice would be to bear in mind that for every second-hand caravan suffering from delamination (or damp, come to that), there will be scores that aren't. Go and buy one of those instead.

- ▶ Check that all the burners on the hob ignite, plus those in the grill and oven, if applicable.

- ▶ Make sure the fridge operates on all its power settings (gas, electricity and, when connected to a towcar, 12-volt).

- ▶ Check the heater works efficiently.

- ▶ Ask for a water supply to be fed into the caravan so you can reassure yourself that the pump works properly and that all the taps reward you with a flow of water when turned on. With water in the system, turn on the water heater – again, if applicable, try it on both its gas and mains electricity settings.

- ▶ Try every light (but don't lose too much sleep if the bulb's gone in one of them).

- ▶ Outside the caravan, make sure that the corner steadies wind up and down smoothly, and that the jockey wheel clamp/winder and handbrake aren't obstructive in use.

- ▶ Check that the electrical plugs are in good condition and that they attach to the relevant sockets on the car with seamless ease. Make sure the cables haven't been chafed by coming into contact with the road when towing. The caravan, if it was made from 2008 onwards, will probably have just one 13-pin socket. That's fine – you can buy an adaptor for your car if it needs it.

- ▶ Have a good look round for any signs of exterior damage, such as dented aluminium panels or cracks in any plastic or glassfibre body parts. Okay, they may just be cosmetic irritants, but what caused the damage in the first place – owner carelessness? Why wasn't the damage put right? If my caravan suffered a cracked plastic cowl on the A-frame, for example, I would have it replaced – whether I were selling it or not. It may just be a sign of someone who hasn't looked after the caravan as well as he or she might, and it should at least put you on your guard for other examples of owner indifference.

- ▶ Cast a careful eye over the entire run of the awning rail (see Chapter 2 for more information on awnings). If this has been damaged in any way, you won't be able to use an awning unless you have the rail repaired or replaced. Just bear in mind, thousands of other used caravans won't have this kind of damage.

- Check the tyres very carefully for signs of damage: cracks in the sidewalls, blistering, flat spots (where the shape of the tyres has become irrevocably deformed due to standing in one position for weeks or months) or erratically worn tread due to over- or under-inflation.

- Even if the tyres look perfectly okay, ask the seller if the caravan has ever had new ones fitted. If the answer is 'No' or 'No idea' and the caravan is four or more years old, you need to factor in the cost of a visit to the local tyre depot for new replacements. The trouble is that caravan tyres will always look like they've just come out of the factory, because they never cover enough mileage to show any signs of wear. And even though they may have travelled just four or five thousand miles, maybe fewer, in seven years, the caravan's tyres have still had seven years' worth of exposure to the elements, with the attendant risk of blistering and cracking – which could result in a blow-out.

- If you're viewing the caravan at a location that makes it impossible to make all the various connections, be realistic.

If you like the look of the caravan enough to want to put an offer in, then do so on the condition that the deal is dependent on everything working as it should. If the caravan is being stored on a compound, say, you can agree the provisional deal and arrange to come and collect it from the owner's house or from a nearby caravan site where you can have the opportunity to try everything out before handing over the deposit.

Key point

If you're buying a caravan from a private seller who is an experienced caravanner, it's a golden opportunity to tap into his or her know-how. Most caravanners will be delighted to take the time to answer all the queries you may have, however trivial you may think they are, and to pass on all the hints and tips they've acquired over the years.

KNOWING WHEN TO WALK AWAY

When you go to look at a second-hand caravan, you must be strong-willed enough to say 'Thanks but no thanks' if there are too many obvious question marks against it (see the checklist above) or if there's just something about it or the seller that doesn't give you confidence. If you have been lucky enough to take someone with you who knows a thing or two about caravans, take their counsel.

The urge to take home the first one you see will no doubt be strong – it's just human nature, after all, and the entire retail industry takes full advantage of it. Whether you're buying a new carpet, a three-piece suite, a Blu-ray player, windows for your house, a car, a caravan – whatever – it's understandable that you want to get it home as quickly as possible so you can start using it. Once you've made the decision that you're going to buy, you can hardly think about anything else.

So here you are, you're looking at this caravan and the chap selling it has told you there's somebody else coming to see it later that afternoon. That immediately makes you feel that you may lose out if you don't do the deal there and then. But that awning rail does look a bit bashed, and although he says he's had it serviced 'fairly regularly', he doesn't have the documentation to prove it.

Walk away. You'll be glad you did when you eventually find a caravan that ticks all the right boxes – which your gut reaction tells you is the one for you and which backs that up by passing your fine-toothed-comb inspection with flying colours. You'll look back on the one with the bent awning rail and shudder at the thought that you nearly bought it before the 'Walk Away' angel alighted on your shoulder and uttered those wise words!

Remember this

Bought your caravan on eBay without having seen it? Definitely not recommended! But you must still reserve the right to walk away if, when you go to collect it, it fails to match up to the description that enticed you to bid for it in the first place. Refusing to pay up may be an uncomfortable experience, but not as uncomfortable as taking ownership of a lemon.

NO SERVICE HISTORY?

There are safety-related mechanisms and equipment on a caravan, not least of which is the braking system. On a motorway or dual carriageway in the UK, you could be cruising perfectly legally and comfortably at 60mph, so you want to know you can bring the outfit to a halt from that speed as quickly as circumstances dictate that you need to.

If the caravan you're thinking of buying has a history that proves regular visits to a service bay, that's a huge bonus because it means the brakes – not only on the road wheels but the handbrake as well – have been checked and adjusted as necessary and that any worn-out parts have been replaced. A service technician will also make sure that the gas system is working as it should be – that, too, offers great peace of mind.

Although you're right to be wary of the lack of a service history, then, it needn't be a deal breaker with a beautifully presented caravan that seems nigh on perfect in most other regards. But do make it a priority to book it in for a service as soon as possible after you've bought it.

MAKING THE MOST OF A WARRANTY

Remember that a dealer's caravans will be more expensive than the equivalent being sold by a private seller – the dealer has to make a profit on the sale. If the caravan in question is an old worthy costing just a few hundred pounds, it may be 'sold as seen', i.e. with no warranty.

But if that's the marketplace in which you're browsing, you'd be as well looking out for a similarly aged/specified caravan from a private seller and using the money you'll save from doing so to go towards repairs or even that vital first service.

If you do buy a caravan that benefits from a warranty, you'll need to use the caravan fairly regularly within the period of the warranty's validity so you can become aware of defects that occur.

However, your first inspection for defects should take place on the forecourt. If you're set on buying the caravan, examine it with forensic precision. You must then ask for any fault you come across – however minor – to be attended to. Common niggles include things like loose cooker or sink lids, ineffective locker stays, and blinds or flyscreens that don't retract properly.

Go ahead and do the deal. Then book a stay on a site fairly local to the dealership on the very day you go to collect your caravan. Arrive at the showroom in the morning, leaving yourself enough time to drive off to your chosen site and set everything up in time for you to call them with any worries or queries you may have before close of business – even if it's simply to ask someone to remind you what that switch on the side of the wardrobe is for.

HOW CAN YOU DATE A CARAVAN?

If it's a 1992 model or younger, it's easy to check, as 1992 is when the Caravan Registration and Identification Scheme (CRiS) was introduced for all caravans manufactured by members of the National Caravan Council, the UK industry body. Luckily, all the major British manufacturers come under the umbrella of the scheme, although most caravans imported from the continent aren't included – unless the owners have taken it on themselves to have their caravans CRiS-registered privately, which is always a possibility.

The 17-digit code that identifies the individual caravan – and its year of manufacture – will be etched clearly on the windows and stamped on the chassis. The seller should be able to show you the accompanying documentation to prove ownership. If either that or etched windows are noticeable by their absence ... well, here's hoping you've got your walking boots on. It could be that the seller really doesn't know how old the caravan is – quite common with older ones – and that '1985 or '86' is his or her honest guess. Ultimately, the caravan's chassis number determines age so, if it's a pre-CRiS model, take a note of this number and contact the manufacturer to confirm what the seller is telling you. If it turns out that '1985 or '86' is actually 1982, it's no big deal but may be a bargaining point in getting a few pounds knocked off the asking price.

Two potential problems: one is that the passage of time may have worn the chassis number away; the other is that the manufacturer in question may have long since been consigned to history.

That's when it becomes difficult to age a caravan with any real accuracy. Acrylic double-glazed windows became the norm in 1978, replacing the almost universally used single-glazed glass; rear fog lamps became mandatory in late 1979 … but there's not a huge amount else to go on.

An expert from one of the many owners' clubs for individual marques may be able to shed some anorak-like light on the subject, but you may just have to accept that a caravan with more than a couple of decades to its name will for ever have to remain of indeterminate age.

To be honest, if your caravan is that old, getting an exact age probably doesn't matter that much.

LIVING WITH A BARGAIN-BASEMENT CARAVAN

Much of the pleasure of caravanning comes from the places you visit, the people you meet, the quality of the sites you stay at, the view of the sunset over a glass of wine, the laughter of the kids – not so much the vintage of the accommodation you use to achieve all this.

The opening paragraphs of this chapter touched on the other benefits of going cheap and cheerful. You can sell the old thing for the same amount of money you paid for it – maybe even more – because really old caravans effectively stop depreciating as long as they're habitable and in more or less one piece. If someone in your area is looking for a cheap four-berther, they'll regard your £600 asking price as a bargain in the same way that you did when you bought it for £500.

We discussed, too, how buying a cheap and cheerful caravan gives you an easy, low-risk way of sampling caravanning. But wouldn't hiring a caravan fulfil the same purpose? Yes, of course it would, but caravan rental is expensive and, at the end of the holiday, you've got to hand it back. With the old thing, you can have a few more enjoyable weekends out of it while you make up your mind which way you want to go – and then sell it or keep it as you think fit.

Rental is a good idea if, say, you're thinking of returning to caravanning after a long lay-off and want to see for yourself whether or not the features crammed into a state-of-the-art tourer justify the high asking price.

When you buy a cheap caravan, it's often from someone who's done exactly as described above and who is moving on to bigger and better things. If you're really lucky, you'll get an awning included in the price because it won't fit the dream machine the seller is moving on to.

Older tourers, bereft of flab-inducing luxury extras, generally weigh a lot less than their more corpulent equivalents from subsequent decades. Your common-or-garden 1970s family-berth caravan will be right at home with your Volkswagen Golf, Citroën C4, Peugeot 307, Ford Focus or Vauxhall Astra.

WHAT DO YOU GET IN A CHEAP CARAVAN?

A local paper picked up at random yielded the following small ad: a 1985 four-berth Ace Ambassador, described as being in good condition; double glazing, fridge, cooker with oven, hot water, full awning with groundsheet … £600.

Then there's a CI Europa three/four-berth (no year given) with mains and 12-volt electrics, hob/grill, heater, new curtains, full and porch awnings, stereo radio/cassette and spare wheel … £750.

Too much? Okay. How about a Piper 1100T two-berth, gas hob/grill, heater and mains electrics … £400. But that Ambassador, with an oven, an awning and hot water? For £600? Not everything is always as good as it seems, but that is an amazing package for that kind of money, and I would certainly be off to have a good look at it at the very least.

Assuming none of the above is on its last legs, it begs the question: why on earth pay any more than this for your first caravan? Live with it initially, at minimal cost, and it may even allow you to go caravanning while you save up like mad for that £15,000 model you want to buy next year (or will it be the year after …?).

Don't forget – leave enough in the kitty for a service and three new tyres. If there's no spare wheel included, buy one from a caravanning accessory shop. Make sure you have a wheelbrace and a suitable jack, too – and practise changing a wheel at home or in your storage compound. You don't want to be making your wheel-changing debut at the side of the A14 in the middle of the Friday afternoon rush hour ...

Of course, there are compromises involved. Don't expect the inside of a 1970s caravan to be the last word in good taste (indeed, it may come as a shock at first if you've never previously entered that nether-world of burnt orange upholstery and nylon curtains with massive, brightly coloured flowers). You'll probably find that even caravans from the following decade haven't stood the interior-décor test of time very well.

NO HOT WATER? IT'S NOT SO BAD

Don't be too surprised if an older caravan doesn't have a hot-water system; there are some brand-new budget models on the market even now that lack this feature. However, in practice, this is less of a burden than you may at first think. After all, if you choose to stay on caravan sites that have dedicated washing-up areas – a great many do – not to mention fully equipped and heated shower blocks, you probably won't miss it that much.

I can't remember the last summer caravanning holiday when I even switched the water heater on. It's a great boon if you're staying on a basic site or rally field but, even then, it's not the end of the world: it's hardly a chore to boil up a pan of water or a kettle if you need a basin of hot water. Indeed, when you put the kettle on for your breakfast cuppa, fill it right up and use the water that's left over to quickly wash up the few breakfast things – job done.

No on-board heater? Treat yourself to a small fan heater with variable power settings and stash it away in a bed-locker, ready to be pressed into service if the evening turns a bit cool.

That brings to mind the one 'luxury' that should be considered an essential when buying a caravan – a mains electricity system. In my opinion, doing without that is one compromise too many.

The upholstery may long since have been unable to provide much in the way of meaningful support; you can add some scatter cushions and bolsters, but your holidays will be that much more comfortable if you have all the soft furnishings reupholstered. Don't forget, most of the pieces will be used as mattresses at night-time, too.

Remember, cheap caravans can – and do – give their owners many reasons to be cheerful.

Buying a brand-new caravan

It's worth bearing in mind that British manufacturers generally launch their new ranges for the year in the previous September, with one or two models kept up their sleeves for the bigger caravan exhibitions that take place every autumn and winter. So, summer – July and August especially – is a good time to seek out a bargain on a brand-new caravan. Dealers will be keen to clear 'last year's' stock as they await the new models. You can't afford to be too choosy if you adopt this strategy, though, because the models on your preferred shortlist may well have sold out long since.

Many bigger dealers promote their own 'specials': caravans branded as their own but which are, in essence, rebadged versions of mainstream models from the caravan manufacturers' own ranges. These can be worthy of serious consideration: a special may have a soft furnishings colour scheme that you think is far better than anything the manufacturer has to offer in its 'official' version, for example; or it may include a host of extra equipment for the same sort of price.

If you decide to go for broke and plough a chunk of your life savings into a brand-new caravan, you may well find yourself starting your research at one of the big caravan shows. There's a compelling case for going to one of these exhibitions – an opportunity to see almost every new caravan under one roof. It's not just British-made caravans you'll find here: there are many different makes of overseas-manufactured tourers imported officially into the UK, and these are always well-represented at the major exhibitions.

Although the exhibition stands are branded under the caravan manufacturers' names, most of them are run largely by sales staff from some of that manufacturer's dealer network. And their job, of course, is to sell you a caravan. There will be killer deals on offer: special show prices that can never be repeated; free alloy wheels and built-in stereos; monogrammed his 'n' hers towels ... temptation everywhere.

All well and good, and most of the dealers will be established businesses, but the one you're about to sign on the dotted line with may be 150 miles from where you live. That's where you'll be collecting the caravan from; that's who your contract is with if you need to consult about warranty work or any other difficulty.

While the dealer seven miles away from your home may not be able to offer the same cut-price deal or free stereo, he's a lot more handily placed for repairs and servicing – and you may find through word of mouth that he has a brilliant reputation locally for looking after his customers. He's certainly the one who would get my business if I were buying a new caravan.

Remember this

Fitted stereo radio/CD players are common on new caravans now, but some are better than others. Don't be dismayed if the manufacturer has provided all the necessary wiring for a head unit and speakers but hasn't provided any hardware. On the contrary, that gives you the opportunity to fit better-quality components. The biggest disappointment is usually cheap, unbranded speakers that offer poor sound quality.

If you decide to buy new:

▶ Don't be afraid to haggle. If the salesperson you're dealing with is convinced that you're going to part with lots of money to buy a new caravan, he or she will be very keen to secure your business and the commission that goes with it.

▶ Even if, despite your best efforts, there's little or no room for manoeuvre on the selling price, try to negotiate goods and/ or services as part of the package. For example: a free first annual service; a free upgrade to more expensive upholstery; free water containers and wheel clamp.

- Make sure any optional extras you've requested – a microwave or a radio/CD player, for example – are noted on the order sheet.

- As with buying a used model, take it away on collection and try it out at a local site. You must identify and report any problem as soon as you can.

BUYING AND LIVING WITH AN OVERSEAS-MANUFACTURED CARAVAN

At the time of writing, there aren't as many continental marques being imported officially into the UK as there were a few years ago, but there's still a wide choice. Some, such as Eriba, Adria and Hymer, have been a familiar part of the scene for a long time. You can even buy an iconic, US-made Airstream in UK-specification now (if you're feeling flush …).

There was, until recently, a clear-cut difference between foreign and British caravans. With the overseas contingent, all had the door on the 'wrong' side; they had voiles (okay, net curtains); they had kitchens on the basic side of basic; they had a big, single window at the front; there wasn't a carpet to be seen; and some of the layouts were decidedly unusual.

That composite description still applies to a lot of foreign caravans, but some manufacturers or importers have taken on board that British caravan buyers, largely speaking, have different needs and desires from their counterparts on the continent. So it is, then, that many overseas-made tourers are made specifically for the UK market, with fully-featured kitchens, loose-fit carpeting and sometimes even with the entrance door on the 'normal' side.

It's not all one-way traffic, though. The very reason that British buyers are drawn to continental caravans in the first place is that the exterior and, more specifically, interior design is refreshingly different, often looking more 'youthful' than the bulk of the offerings from home-grown manufacturers. Well, that too has changed – and design influences from mainland Europe can be clearly seen in many present-day British-made models.

As an example of this, you don't need to look any further than the all-conquering permanent end-bedroom layout (of which more in Chapter 3), which was a staple of continental caravan design long before UK manufacturers decided to give it a try. They've never looked back from that. You can now also buy home-grown caravans with features such as 'garages' – exterior-access compartments with a door big enough to lift bikes and other bulky outdoor gear into.

Build quality has long been a factor. A lot of continental caravans are made from chunky, thick-gauge aluminium panels that feel bulletproof to the touch. Inside, it's not unusual to encounter furniture that comes across as being equally indestructible, with thick-set wood much in evidence. The inevitable weightiness that results from using such substantial materials is often offset by the minimalist interiors, meaning that you can tow a lot of well-made, continental four-berth caravans quite easily with a car such as a Ford Focus or Peugeot 307 – a feat that British makers find hard to match.

Mind you, if you marry the Forth Bridge-type construction with a multi-berth layout and a fully kitted-out, British-style equipment roster, you end up with a hefty beast that can't be towed by anything this side of a 4 × 4 – and there are certainly a few foreign caravans that fall into this category.

Not so long ago, one could present a convincing argument that most overseas-made caravans were better made than British models, but that's no longer true. To give them credit, UK manufacturers accepted that just one criterion, build quality, was losing them sales in growing numbers. My work involves me crawling in and under more caravans than is probably healthy, and I can say with some confidence that the build quality of British-made caravans is now, for the most part, very good.

At the time of writing, three of the biggest names in the industry – Swift Group, Explorer Group and Bailey – have now adopted new, state-of-the-art construction methods that are claimed to offer increased strength and near-total imperviousness to water ingress. Respectively, these methods are called SMART, SoLid and Alu-Tech.

ARE YOU SITTING COMFORTABLY?

Potential buyers should look closely at imported caravans and ask the question: 'Will I be able to get really comfortable in this?' Many continental caravans just don't do comfort. There's a good reason for this. Typically, Dutch, Belgian, French or German families use the caravan in summer, possibly for the whole season. They hitch up and head south, populating the hundreds of holiday sites spread along the sun-kissed French Atlantic coast, the Costa Verde and the Mediterranean.

They get up in the morning, have breakfast in the awning or outside, go out for the entire day, have a barbecue when they get back in the evening and then go to bed. The seats in the caravan are probably hardly, if ever, used – apart from when they're turned into beds at night-time.

Granted, that's stereotyping somewhat, but it does go some way towards explaining why the 'lounges' in some continental caravans are barely worthy of the name, with seating that can leave you feeling more 'perched'. Often, there's a massive table permanently in situ, which you may sometimes wish you could move somewhere else for a while. Some owners take this to extremes and remove it completely, leaving it behind in the garage.

Of course, not all overseas-made caravans are like that, by any means, but if you like to kick off your shoes at the end of a hard day's holidaying, put your feet up with a glass of wine and sink into a comfy corner, it's just something to be aware of.

Remember this

That 'comfy corner' test is a really important one to try out. Take the family along when you go to look at a caravan, kick your shoes off and get comfortable – if you can. If you can't, well ...

Focus points

The main points to remember from this chapter are:

✱ Give serious consideration to buying a cheap, older 'starter' caravan to see how caravanning suits you.

✱ Most caravans, even the most basic models, will have all the essential amenities for comfortable, relaxed holidays.

✱ If you buy a used caravan, have its gas system safety-checked by a qualified technician.

✱ Familiarize yourself with the symptoms of water ingress (damp) and floor delamination and avoid any caravan thus afflicted.

✱ Unless you're convinced you won't be able to find anything better, don't rush straight in and buy the first caravan you see.

✱ Low-cost second-hand caravans in decent, serviceable condition rarely depreciate. When the time comes to trade up to something newer, you should recoup your initial outlay.

✱ High summer is a good time to negotiate a substantial discount when buying a brand-new caravan.

✱ Buying a caravan from a respected dealer with a good reputation for customer service can pay dividends.

✱ Do investigate continental-built caravans when you're doing your research – many offer a bit of difference that may appeal to you ...

✱ ... but do satisfy yourself that the seating/lounging arrangements offer the comfort that you and your family need.

2

Awnings and accessories

In this chapter, you will learn:

► *all about awnings – how to decide which type is best for you*

► *which other accessories should be on your list of essentials*

► *why one of the cheapest accessories you will ever buy is worth its weight in gold.*

The world of awnings

After the caravan itself, the awning is the most expensive purchase most owners will make – but it's without doubt the most useful. If you're going to use your caravan for more than just weekends away, you really should do yourself a favour and buy an awning for it.

An awning is basically a three-sided tent that attaches to your caravan's sidewall on the door side. Every caravan has an awning rail to form this essential attachment, so you'll certainly be able to find an awning for your particular model.

Chat about awnings to any retailer and the first thing you'll probably be told is that fitting one doubles at a stroke the amount of living space offered by your caravan. But even though you may hear it time and again, it doesn't make it any less true – having an awning enhances no end the pleasure you'll get from your caravan, so it's no wonder that the overwhelming majority of caravan owners invest in one. Take a look around any busy caravan site and you'll hardly see a single caravan unadorned by one.

And, yes, you can treat it as something of an investment in that – unlike virtually every other caravanning accessory – you will at least be able to recoup some of the cost if you sell it on.

Don't be intimidated by the prospect of erecting a big awning. Most retailers have in-house experts who will talk you through, even show you, the setting-up procedure. If you're inheriting an awning from the seller of a used caravan, ask him or her to do the same for you.

Many awnings feature colour-coded or numbered poles to simplify the process, and owners often devise their own colour-coding system once they've erected and dismantled their awning a couple of times. Buying your first-ever awning a couple of days before you go off on a fortnight's holiday and then attempting to erect it for the first time in the full glare of everybody on your site in the south of France is a spectacularly bad idea. Therefore ...

Speaking of which, the next thing you should do is take the caravan off to a quiet site and practise putting the awning up. Stick a bottle of something nice in the fridge while you're doing it as a reward for afterwards. Stay cool, take your time, start again if you need to – when you've done it once, you've cracked it!

Don't rush into buying an awning. Use your caravan on its own a few times so you can get a clearer picture of the type of unit that's going to suit your needs best, because there's an enormous choice on offer. Splash out too soon on a £1,200 mega-awning the size of a tennis court and you may find yourself rattling around in it a bit.

You may wish you'd held back a while and gone for a more compact porch awning or (slightly bigger) midi-awning. Not only are these far quicker to erect and put away again (unlike a full-size awning, you could probably erect these single-handed), they still free up an awful lot of space. Muddy shoes can be discarded here (indeed, you can keep all the outdoor footwear here), you can hang all the coats up, stash the crates of beer, bring the outdoor chairs in at night, use it as a sun lounge and so on. These more modestly sized units are highly useful and versatile add-ons – some can be extended by attaching an annexe. Also, porch and midi-awnings will transfer readily to a different caravan, as they'll fit just about anything.

You can go even more basic: if all you really need is somewhere to sit outside in the shade, a sun canopy would be a good option for about £70–£150. And if you're really anti erecting anything, you can attach a 'roller' version of a canopy to the side of your caravan. Pitch up, roll it out, peg it down: instant shade.

ADDING ANOTHER BEDROOM

However, if you intend using the awning for entertaining and/ or family meals, you'll benefit hugely from all the space that a full-width unit brings. Some can be made even bigger by means of an annexe, which can also be made more snug by fitting it out with an inner tent, giving you a really nice extra bedroom. This is a feature much appreciated by 'I want my own space' teenagers enjoying those last couple of holidays with mum and dad before they go off backpacking around Australia for three years or whatever it is that teenagers do these days!

It also gives you a realistic alternative to selling your caravan if, for whatever reason – expanding family, children wanting to bring a friend on holiday, grandchildren now old enough to come away with you – you realize that you need more berths occasionally. Whether you buy the annexe now or add it later is up to you, but awnings are like any other item of equipment – this year's big bargain could be next year's discontinued line, and accessories may become harder to get hold of.

You also need to consider the material you want to lay on the ground inside the awning. Many caravan sites frown on the use of a traditional, tent-like groundsheet on a grass pitch – it's non-breathable and leaves the grass all horrible and yellow. And when the site's busy, there's little chance of the grass getting time to recover.

Breathable, washable awning carpet is widely available, and as well as making the site staff happier, it does make your awning look a bit posher, too.

Lots of caravans have an external mains point that lives under a weather-protected flap on the sidewall or just inside an exterior hatch – a facility much appreciated by awning owners. As long as you're not overloading the site's electricity supply (see Chapter 7 for more on this), you can keep the awning warm on cooler nights with a little fan heater, not to mention banishing younger members of the family out there with their own TV.

Remember this

Some caravans higher up the food chain come with a built-in awning warmer. This is basically an extension of the caravan's blown-air heating system, with a covered outlet on the sidewall. I remember thinking it seemed a bit gimmicky when I first saw one – but it's actually surprisingly effective.

There are three things to bear in mind when doing your research before buying an awning.

1 Every awning, no matter what its cost, will reward the conscientious owner. If you maintain it and treat it properly, you'll get many years' service from it.

2 Think about whether or not you're likely to change caravans sometime during the life of your awning. You may care to check when buying your awning what ranges of tourers it would be suitable for in its particular size.

3 Generally speaking, you get what you pay for. It almost goes without saying that a big, top-of-the-range awning costing £1,800 will have a lot more features and better detailing than a similarly sized one costing £600. If you want to take advantage of attributes such as mud skirts around the base, waterproof stitching and heavy-duty reinforcing at pressure points, you may have to consider going upmarket.

When you go shopping, ask a knowledgeable salesperson to point out the detailing that makes awning 'A' so much more expensive than awning 'B' in the opposite corner of the showroom. If you're likely to use the awning just a couple of times a year for longer breaks – during your main summer holiday and a half-term week, say – awning 'B' will probably suit you just fine.

WHAT SIZE OF AWNING DO YOU NEED?

Sizing your awning is straightforward. You should be able to get this so-called A–B measurement from your caravan handbook or from the manufacturer's website (the specification charts in

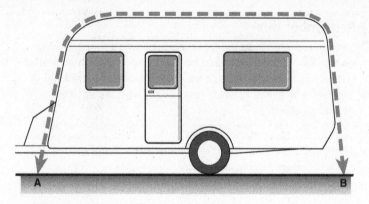

Figure 2.1 Awning A–B measurement.

sales brochures usually always include awning sizes). Otherwise, it'll take you just a few minutes with a piece of string or wool, a tape measure and a couple of drawing pins.

Use one of the drawing pins to secure the string to the ground directly underneath one end of your caravan's awning rail, then thread it through the rail until it reaches the ground directly underneath the other end of the rail. The length of that piece of string is your caravan's A–B measurement. That's really all there is to it.

WHAT ARE THEY MADE OF?

Synthetic materials are predominant in the world of awnings; once upon a time it was cotton, but it's hardly used nowadays.

Acrylic is widely employed in awning manufacture, finding favour for its hard-wearing properties and colour fastness. If left uncoated, it can 'breathe', making it a particularly good choice for bedroom use. Lighter polyester (often coated with PVC or polyurethane) is often used to provide a leak-free roof panel.

When it comes to frames, your choice of materials is steel, glassfibre or aluminium. Steel is the cheapest and the heaviest – and its sturdiness means it will last for many years, even though it will need to be well looked after to keep it rust-free.

Lightweight aluminium (about half the weight of steel) and glassfibre are rustproof, maintenance-free alternatives. You may be able to upgrade an awning by specifying aluminium poles instead of the steel ones that come as standard.

Don't forget to take account of the weight of the awning and any additional accessories you buy for it. It's important that you don't exceed the maximum payload allocation for your caravan and/or the ability of your car to tow it (see Chapter 4).

The bigger the awning, the more susceptible it is to damage from really high winds, so do take account of any unfavourable weather forecasts. Better to delay putting the awning up by a day or so than to risk torn fabric or bent poles.

Key point

It's worth knowing what the weather's going to be up to as the end of your holiday approaches. If the last couple of days look like they're going to be showery, better to dismantle your awning and pack it away when it's still dry. If circumstances dictate that you do have to pack away a damp awning, unpack it again as soon as you can when you get home and allow it to dry out – this is also a good opportunity to give it a thorough clean.

The other accessories you can't live without

Once you've bought your caravan, you'll no doubt find yourself browsing caravanning websites, leafing through the specialist magazines and browsing the shelves of the caravan accessories shop, tempted by all those amazing gadgets you never even knew existed but which you most certainly can't live without.

The truth is, you can get by quite happily with a handful of must-have items, some of which will be included with your caravan. If you're buying a second-hand model, you may, as previously mentioned, be lucky enough to inherit the whole lot in one go. Don't leave home without the following.

▶ Leisure battery

This powers most of your caravan's lights, the water pump and the spark-ignition on the cooker (if so equipped). When connected to the site mains supply, most caravans have a built-in charger that keeps your battery topped up ready to be used when you're not connected to an electricity supply.

▶ Mains lead

This will be supplied with a brand-new caravan. If you need to buy one, make sure it's 25 metres long. In most cases, your mains connection point will be substantially closer than that, but you'll be glad of its length one day. While you're buying it, you may as well shell out a few pounds more on a domestic adaptor that connects to a mains socket in your house. Attach your mains lead to this and your caravan can have an electricity supply while parked in your drive – handy if you're using it as an impromptu guest bedroom, or even to get the fridge up and running while you're loading up the caravan.

▶ Water containers

You'll need one to accommodate your fresh-water supply and at least one for your waste or 'grey' water to drain into. Water is devilishly heavy, so choose containers that can be wheeled or rolled.

Some waste-water containers are shaped to give a 'piggy back' to a toilet cassette, the idea being that you can wheel both over to their respective emptying points – sound in theory and practice. You'll also need a short length of grey or black ribbed hose for each waste-water outlet from your caravan (probably two).

Remember this

You'll probably see other caravanners on site who have two fresh-water containers sitting outside their caravan – one connected to the water system and one as a back-up. This does ensure continuity of supply: fill up both containers when you arrive and connect one. When that runs dry, plonk the submersible pump in the other one straight away, then go and fill up the empty one and keep that in reserve ... and so it goes on.

▶ Step

Every new caravan will be supplied with a step, although the chances are it won't be the heaviest-duty one you've ever seen. You may choose to upgrade to a more substantial one.

Remember this

Treating yourself to new accessories and gadgets every now and then is undoubtedly one of the pleasures of caravanning. But don't forget to take account of any additional weight. This is especially important if you're already running your caravan close to its maximum laden weight (MTPLM).

▶ Wheel clamp and hitch lock

The minimum anti-theft protection you should consider is to fit a wheel clamp and a hitch lock. As well as a big, heavy-duty wheel clamp to fit to the caravan when it's on site or in storage, I strongly recommend that you also invest in a smaller one – one that can be whipped on and off in seconds – for use at quick stopovers, such as coffee breaks at motorway service areas. See Chapter 8 for more details.

▶ Levelling blocks/wheel chocks

Most of the time, your caravan will be pitched nice and level, but sometimes it won't be. These cheap blocks (or ramps), which can be stored unobtrusively in your caravan's front exterior locker, effect a simple cure. Use in conjunction with a spirit level. See also Chapter 7.

▶ Spare wheel

What a shame a spare wheel isn't included as standard with every new caravan. Don't risk taking your caravan anywhere without one – not even the trip home from picking it up.

Remember this

Just like your car's spare tyre, the caravan's spare is often forgotten about when owners check and adjust tyre pressures. Making sure you always attend to the spare as well is a very good habit to get into – finding out that it's dangerously under-inflated when you need to use it means you're still stranded, unless you have a foot pump in the boot of the car.

▶ Jack/wheel brace/torque wrench

This little trilogy goes hand-in-hand with the spare wheel. Familiarize yourself with your caravan's jacking points and make sure the jack you buy has a sufficient weight limit to accommodate your caravan. The torque wrench is the only way to be certain that you've tightened up the wheel nuts correctly (the wheel nuts' torque settings will be in the caravan handbook and, in some enlightened cases, stamped on the wheel arch of the caravan itself).

▶ Toilet chemicals

Buy in bulk. You do not want to be in a caravan that has run out of toilet chemicals – honestly, you don't.

▶ Towing mirrors

Buy three: one for each door mirror on your car and one spare. Make sure that the type you buy will fit your car's mirror casing. The most widely used towing mirrors – or extension mirrors – are those with adjustable arms and rubber straps that fit around the car mirror casing. They'll fit most 'conventional' car mirrors.

I like the type with a single metal bar and clamps that secure the unit to the top of the door mirror casing (Figure 2.2). Be very careful to make sure it is tightly attached – and be obsessive in your quest not to lose the little rubber 'feet' that protect the surface of the car mirror. This is much easier said than done.

▶ DiY/gardening gloves and rubber mat

Keep these in your caravan's external front locker or in the boot of the car, ready to be pressed into service when hitching up or uncoupling. The gloves will give you a bit more purchase

Figure 2.2 Looking back: extension mirrors are essential when towing a caravan.

in your battle against recalcitrant winders and clamps, not to mention protection when handling muddy, grimy jockey wheel stanchions.

The mat gives you something to kneel on when connecting the caravan's electrical plugs to car sockets that may not be the last word in accessibility.

▶ Plastic towball cover

Possibly the cheapest caravanning accessory there is, but it punches way above its weight by ensuring you don't get grease on your trousers if you brush against the towball while reaching into the boot. The best 99p you'll ever spend? Very likely.

Remember this

You know the heavy-duty paper mats that mechanics put in your car footwells when it goes in for a service? Don't chuck them away. Keep them rolled up in your caravan's gas locker or somewhere else easily accessible and use them to protect its carpet or flooring if you're loading it when it's wet or muddy outside. Two or three doormats from the pound shop will do the job, too.

Focus points

The main points to remember from this chapter are:

✳ An awning will increase the amount of living space dramatically.

✳ Be certain of what you want to use the awning for before going out to buy one – no need to buy an enormous, top-of-the-range model if all you want is somewhere to keep wellies and coats and maybe a spare fridge.

✳ Your caravan handbook will tell you what its awning measurements are. Otherwise, carry out the A–B measurement explained in this chapter.

✳ You can add a bedroom annexe to an awning instead of trading up to a caravan with more beds.

✳ Ask the salesperson to show you how to erect your chosen awning. Try it for yourself on a quiet site before its first 'proper' outing.

✳ Make sure the weight of the awning, when added to your payload, keeps you within your permitted limit.

✳ Dismantle the awning a day or so early if the weather forecast isn't great. Avoid packing away a wet awning if you can.

✳ If your caravan doesn't have a spare wheel, buy one before you tow it anywhere (plus a suitable jack and wheel brace).

✳ Buy three towing mirrors for your car, keeping one as a spare.

✳ Don't forget that towball cover!

3

Choosing the right layout

In this chapter, you will learn:

▶ *why it's important to choose the layout that's right for you*

▶ *the pros and cons of the most popular configurations*

▶ *why permanent bedrooms have become such a hit.*

Choosing a caravan with the wrong layout is a common mistake – and an expensive one to put right. The only way round it is to bite hard on the bullet and sell the caravan, probably costing you thousands of pounds in the process if the vehicle in question is a new one. Here's a cautionary tale that illustrates the point perfectly.

Case study

Geoff Keen, a caravanner of many, many years' standing, had gone to one of the big annual exhibitions and been seduced by a new model sporting the (then) very much in-vogue L-shaped front lounge with deep picture window and an aura of open space that completely bowled his wife and him over.

The soft lighting of the display model, the even softer charm of the salesman and the thought of sitting in the evening with a bottle of wine looking at the sun set over the shimmering sea through the deep picture window that's a common feature on L-shapes – all did the trick. They bought the caravan on the spot.

It was only a matter of weeks before disillusionment set in – they really didn't like their new caravan. On their very first time away in it, they realized that there was nowhere convenient to put the tea and biscuits, due to the L-shape sofa precluding the fitment of the front chest of drawers they had been so used to over the course of the decades.

They realized that much of the so-called seating area of the L-shape sofa was actually too uncomfortable to sit on – a real problem when they asked some friends from a neighbouring caravan in for a few drinks.

In short, they couldn't relax when they went away in the caravan. Of course, that pretty much defeats the object of caravanning, so the Keens had no choice but to go back to the dealer and trade in the 'wrong' caravan for the one they should have bought in the first place. Their mistake cost them £5,000.

Every caravan layout is a compromise – it's just that some are less of a compromise than others, and it's your job to consider every square inch of the model you're thinking of buying to minimize any potential irritations that, like Chinese water torture, will start off as an 'oh-well-never-mind' niggle and develop into the sort of scenario outlined above.

In that instance, it was an L-shape front lounge that was the kiss of death. It could just have easily been a huge end-washroom that ate up far too much living space; or a double bed that the kids refused to share after a first, fractious holiday; or a caravan with just one place to put the TV (and it's not where you would have put it).

You owe it to yourself to do as much research as possible into which of the many layouts – the number of which has soared with the introduction of so many continental caravans in the past few years – suits you and your family best.

You literally need to get everyone over to the showroom or the exhibition hall and have them sit on the seats and lie on the beds. If you can't all get comfortable on the seats or if the beds are too narrow, you need to find out while your cheque book is still safely in your pocket.

And so on. The choice of layout is a scarily easy one to get wrong, so here we'll consider all the most popular options and go through the potential pros and cons that you need to weigh up.

Points to consider

▶ How many of you will be using the caravan? It's not as easy as just homing in on two-berth models for couples, three-berthers for two-plus-child and so on. As we'll see, a six-berth caravan can be a fantastic choice as accommodation for three or four, and most five-berth models, with a lounge/bedroom at either end, are excellent two-berthers.

▶ Many older children like the adventure of sleeping in a bedroom annexe attached to an awning or in a small tent pitched alongside the caravan (a pup tent). It's well worth bearing this in mind if you find that your heart's set on a particular layout that doesn't have enough berths on board.

▶ Some caravan washrooms are lavish affairs that compare favourably with an en-suite facility in a hotel; it's easy to be impressed by them. But a big washroom takes up a huge amount of precious space for an amenity that may not see an awful lot of use. Wouldn't a longer front lounge or a more spacious kitchen area be much more user-friendly? You need to be hard-headed when making your choice.

▶ When you try the caravan in the showroom, sit in the lounge and imagine you're settling down for the evening after a tiring day. Is it good and comfortable? Can you get into a comfy position without clashing feet? Is there enough room for everyone?

Remember this

If you intend to pitch a pup tent alongside the caravan, contact the site first to make sure that (a) it does actually allow tents to be erected and (b) your pitch will be sufficiently roomy for you to do so. Some sites don't allow tents at all, while others are happy to accept pup tents, which they may define as a tent that's too small to stand upright in.

L-SHAPE FRONT LOUNGES

The more conventional layout in this part of a caravan is a pair of parallel sofas with a central chest of drawers/table top right at the front. We've touched on L-shape front lounges (or dinettes, as they're often referred to), but now let's look at them in a bit more detail. The L-shape in question is the configuration of the sofa, which runs alongside the front nearside wall, forward of the entrance door, and under the front window of the caravan. This allows the fitment of a deeper-than-usual 'picture' window on the offside wall. L-shape options are available in two- or multi-berth caravans.

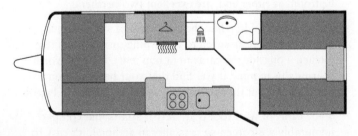

Figure 3.1 An L-shape front lounge layout.

Pros

▶ Lots of initial wow-factor when you first walk in the door. The L-shape front lounges are invariably stunning to look at.

▶ Many have a deeper picture window on the offside that is a real bonus if the view is especially picturesque.

Cons

▶ Some may find that there's a lack of comfortable seating locations. The section along the nearside wall is great, allowing feet-up wallowing in either corner but, invariably, it all goes a bit wrong along by the front window. The depth of the squab (the part of the seat that accommodates your bottom and upper legs) is usually less, imparting a slightly 'perched' feel that's far from comfortable, and if you're taller than 5'9" or so, the back of your head will probably be in close contact with a curtain rail or pelmet.

▶ You may be in luck and find that there's a shelf or worktop on which you can sit your tea, coffee or glass of wine, but factor a tray of biscuits, bowl of olives or some cheese and crackers into the equation and you'll be struggling. You'll have to bring the freestanding table into play from its store (most caravans have a bespoke cabinet for this very purpose).

▶ That thought may not faze you one bit and that's fine, but the presence of the aforementioned front chest in the parallel-seating layout relegates the use of the freestanding table to set mealtimes only. It's just one less thing to do, isn't it?

▶ At night, an L-shape sofa transforms via pull-out slats to become a double bed only – its very shape rules out the option of single beds. Again, that may be of little consequence, but what if you fancy a quick, feet-up snooze in the middle of the afternoon after a long journey? Well, at least one of you will be all right …

Quite often, the L-shape version of a particular model will be available as an option in addition to parallel sofas. It's clearly something you need to think long and hard about before choosing which box to tick on the order form.

CARAVANNING ICON: THE FRONT CHEST OF DRAWERS

This is the piece of furniture that sits right at the front of the caravan between two parallel sofas. It's a front layout that's almost as old as caravanning itself, but it has survived the passage of time because of its sheer user-friendliness.

As well as the obvious storage benefits of having a chest of drawers, the table top has a multitude of uses (writing postcards, accommodating coffee cups, providing a home for the TV), and because its area can be expanded by sliding out, there's rarely a need to go to the trouble of fetching the big, cumbersome freestanding table from its store.

Some cheaper parallel-sofa caravans don't have this chest, and nor do those with L-shape lounges or wrap-around seating. This latter configuration is a definite case of 'try before you buy'. The section of wrap-around seating that runs along by the front window is, as mentioned before, hardly ever comfortable.

Permanent double-bed caravans

Although overwhelmingly sold to couples, the majority of permanent double-bed (PDB) caravans are actually four-berth models: as well as the permanent double bed at the back, the front lounge makes up into another double (or a pair of singles if the caravan has sufficient body length to accommodate them). Some larger caravans offer a permanent double bed in a six-berth

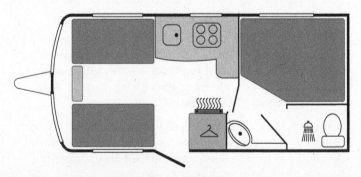

Figure 3.2 A layout with a permanent double bed.

layout, with the usual sofas that convert to a bed at the front and a side-dinette that offers two more (single facing seats that convert into a bed, and a pull-out overhead bunk).

The PDB layout is the caravanning success story of recent times. At the time of writing, it accounts for half of all the caravans sold by one of the UK's biggest manufacturers, and shows no sign of losing its pre-eminence.

Pros

▶ It's no secret why this particular layout is one of the most enduringly popular. In a nutshell, you have a bedroom with a 'proper', permanently sited double bed that does away with the unseemly wrestling match with slabs of upholstery and pull-out slats every night and morning. Some caravans offer the same facility with two single beds.

▶ Just think: at the start of the holiday you simply slip on a fitted sheet, throw on a nice duvet and top it all off with a couple of fluffy pillows and that old teddy bear you've had since you were so high, and that's it. At night-time, when your eyes are heavy with tiredness after a long day out, you can just fall into that big, luxurious bed.

▶ More often than not, the bedroom will be en-suite, with a loo/ shower cubicle enclosed in the corner and a 'hand basin-cum-dressing area' in the body of the room itself. Again, that's the icing on the cake for many couples.

▶ Some models have a so-called island double bed with walk-around access on either side, with an opulent, full-width washroom right at the back. Invariably, these are beautiful caravans to behold, but you need to be absolutely certain that you're happy with so much space being taken up by the combined activities of sleeping and abluting. You may set out with every intention of showering regularly in the caravan – but unless you're a regular visitor to sites with no amenity block, it's a bit extravagant.

▶ A PDB layout that's well worth considering features a transverse permanent double bed at the back – or, more recently, at the front – of the caravan. Because the bed faces across the way, it doesn't intrude into the body of the caravan quite so much, meaning you may benefit from a longer front lounge, or a washroom with a separate shower compartment towards the centre of the caravan.

► There's an enormous amount of storage space under the double bed, often accessible via a hatch from the outside.

► There's a huge amount of choice – every major manufacturer has several PDB caravans, which cover a wide price range.

Cons

► Unless it's a bigger, twin-axle caravan, the fact that there's a substantial bedroom at the back usually means that the rest of the interior is a bit more compact than usual, even though a slightly stubby front lounge won't be much of an issue if there are only two of you lounging in it at any given time. However, the inability to put your feet up and stretch out may disappoint.

► They're not much good as family caravans, especially en-suite models. The position of the loo means that anybody occupying one of the beds in the front lounge will effectively be tiptoeing into your bedroom if he or she happens to get caught short in the night.

Remember this

The quality of the mattresses used on permanent double beds varies. In my experience, the caravan manufacturers usually get it about right, but some mattresses aren't firm enough for my liking.

Some very recent caravans now feature 'memory foam'-type mattresses that are just fantastic – the last example I tried was better than the one we have at home! It's yet another thing to subject to a good test before you buy. While doing so, watch out for other comfort-related aspects, such as the position of the overhead reading lights – some can be annoyingly close to your head or shoulder when sitting up in bed.

Four-berth permanent single-beds caravans

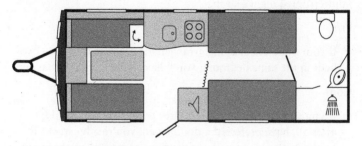

Figure 3.3 A layout with permanent single beds.

Much of what has been written above about permanent double-bed caravans applies to this more recent arrival on the scene. The permanent single-beds (PSB) configuration, although nominally four-berth, is also intended for couples.

The conventional front lounge converts into a double bed in the usual way. At the back, the en-suite bedroom consists of two single beds running parallel to the sidewalls. The best ones look terrific, giving the ambience of a nice hotel twin room – albeit a rather small one.

There's a clear – and growing – demand for this layout. Put simply, the PSB caravan mirrors the arrangement that many couples of a certain age have at home. There comes a time when it's just more comfortable and convenient for a couple to have a bed each while still sharing a room – perhaps because one of them has to keep getting up in the night.

In many caravan double-beds, the occupant further away from the aisle has to negotiate his or her way past his or her partner to get out of (and back into) bed. It can be a clumsy manoeuvre at the best of times and downright awkward if your mobility isn't quite what it used to be.

So it's easy to understand how the PSB caravan is seen as a godsend by many: they get the luxury and convenience of the bespoke bedroom as well as the promise of a good, uninterrupted night's sleep.

Pros

▶ If your preferred sleeping arrangement at home is to have two beds in the same bedroom, you'll be delighted with this layout.

Cons

▶ If you should decide at some later point that you would, after all, have preferred a double bed, you're a bit stuck! If you're happy to do without the permanent-bed arrangement, any caravan with front sofas long enough to make two good single beds will do the trick – and still give you the flexibility of having a double if you wish.

Figure 3.4 A typical permanent single-bed layout.

Two-berth end-washroom models

This is a long-established layout that finds favour with couples who use a lot of basic sites or rally fields that are devoid of toilet/showering facilities. Like all two-berth layouts, nowadays it plays second fiddle to the all-conquering permanent-bed four-berth tourers that, as we've seen, are de facto two-berthers.

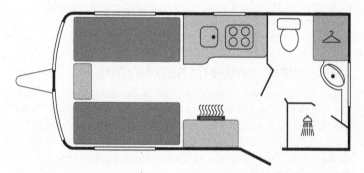

Figure 3.5 Typical layout of a two-berth end-washroom model.

Pros

▶ Totally self-sufficient layout, ideal for caravanners who attend a lot of club meets or rallies with minimal on-site facilities.

▶ Lounges are usually long enough to offer a choice of two single beds or a big double.

▶ Two-berth caravans are often compact and relatively lightweight, making them an attractive proposition if your car is also of modest proportions (see Chapter 4 for more on outfit matching).

Cons

▶ There may not be a queue of buyers outside your door when the time comes to sell – it's not the most in-demand layout.

▶ There's no flexibility in the number of people it can sleep. Granted, many potential buyers will regard that as a huge 'pro', but if, say, a grandchild should decide he or she wants

to come caravanning with you, you'll need to look to the
awning for extra accommodation.

Remember this

Many owners of end-washroom two-berthers use the on-board shower
more often than average. For people like them, the increasingly common
fitment of fully sealed shower compartments is good news, because it
lowers the risk of the caravan suffering from problems with damp as
time goes on.

Two-berth end-kitchen layout

This one's becoming something of an endangered species. They
are still out there, but many manufacturers have dropped them
due to lack of demand. They have their aficionados, though:
for instance, keen cooks like the fact that 'their' galley is right
at the back of the caravan, well away from any interference
from up front …

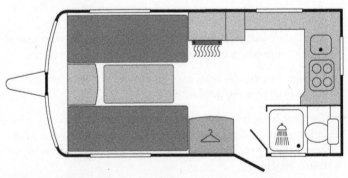

Figure 3.6 A two-berth end-kitchen layout.

On the downside, the fact that there's so much heavy kitchen
equipment this far back isn't ideal for ensuring an evenly laden
caravan when towing.

Four-berth side-dinettes

Figure 3.7 Four-berth side-dinette.

The overhead bunk unit folds unobtrusively against the wall when not in use; the ground-level bed becomes two single seats in daytime mode.

In other words, the usual lounge at the front, two single seats facing each other on one side, the kitchen opposite and a washroom at the back. The side-dinette has a bunk that sits unobtrusively flush against the wall when not in use and takes two minutes to fold out and set up. A curtain wraps around this area to provide some privacy at night.

Top bunks in caravans always carry a weight restriction, typically of between 10 and 11 stone.

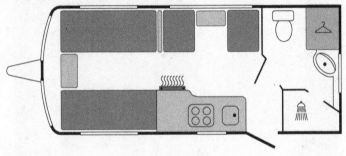

Figure 3.8 A four-berth side-dinette layout.

Pros

▶ This layout is well worth considering for use as a two-berth. It gives couples the wherewithal to make up the front bed and still have a seating area (for example, if you're going out for the evening and don't want to start making a bed up when you return).

▶ The side-dinette has a clip-on table between the seats, which provides welcome extra kitchen workspace – often at a premium in caravans, regardless of layout. It even allows you the luxury of being able to sit down while you work (well, you are on holiday, after all).

Cons

▶ When the side bunks are in use, the occupants are right next to the front lounge – something of a distraction for adults and children if anyone wants to sit up for a while after the rest of the family have gone to bed.

Key point

It's worth remembering that in caravans with one or more pull-out bunks, the sections of upholstery that make up the mattress (often stored in the wardrobe or in a bed locker) may be intended to fit the lower bunk(s), with the upholstery on the lower seats fitting the overhead ones.

Remember this

If a caravan with this layout is being used as a three-berth, the overhead bunk can be removed completely and left behind in the garage, resulting in a considerable weight-saving. On the other hand, you can make up the bunk in the usual way and press it into service as a capacious storage area.

Five-berth twin-dinettes

This is the classic family caravan layout, with a seating area at either end of the caravan (both of which convert into bedrooms), a central kitchen on one side and a washroom on the other. On many models, the rear bedroom closes off by means of a hinged, solid partition – great for giving the occupants their own 'space'.

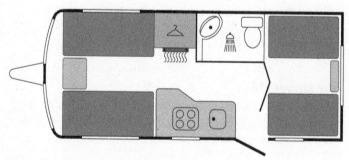

Figure 3.9 A five-berth twin-dinette layout.

On some models, the rear bedroom has its own mains socket, giving the occupants the means to power a Blu-ray/DVD player or games console, charge a mobile phone overnight or boost lighting with a table lamp.

Pros

▶ At night-time, the children are at the opposite end of the caravan from the front lounge. No, it's not a great distance but it does make a difference.

▶ Yet again, this is a superb alternative two-berth. The rear double can be left made up as a 'semi-permanent' bed, but with the flexibility to swap it back to a seating area again whenever you feel like it. Or, should you wish to bring guests caravanning with you, you have a ready-made spare bedroom.

▶ This is also a highly efficient four-berth caravan, especially if one of the two children is a teenager on a seemingly never-ending growth spurt who would therefore appreciate having that roomy double bed to him (or her) self.

Cons

▶ Paradoxically, this configuration may not be the best solution to sleep five. The rear bedroom can consist of a double bed with a single overhead bunk, so there may be disquiet in certain quarters about having to share a bed with a sibling.

▶ The only way to access the bunk when the double bed is made up is to climb up from or down on to the bed. Otherwise, a ladder is provided.

Remember this

If the kids do have to share the space on a double bed, the best bet is often to give them their own sleeping bags and place them 'head to toe'. This gives them at least some independence, however modest!

Fixed rear-bunk six-berth caravans

These were once a relative rarity, but there's now a good choice from several manufacturers. If you are caravanning with a family of six, an awning of some description is essential so you can all spread out a bit.

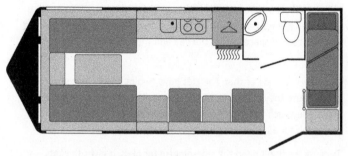

Figure 3.10 A fixed rear-bunk six-berth layout.

This layout features the usual sofas that make up into two single beds or a double at the front, with a side-dinette (fold-out, overhead bunk) and both the kitchen and washroom on the opposite wall. A pair of fixed bunks run transversely across the rear wall.

An alternative layout offers a compact double bed in the side-dinette and two parallel single beds at the back.

There is another layout that's similar to the five-berth twin-dinette, but with two overhead bunks at the rear and the choice of either two singles or a double underneath.

But it's the fixed-bunk six-berther that's considered by many families to be very nearly the perfect four-berth caravan. Here's the opinion of one convert.

Case study

Two years ago, Bill and Cathy MacCorquodale bought a six-berth caravan with fixed bunks along the rear wall as the ideal solution to their touring needs when caravanning with their 11-year-old son and eight-year-old daughter.

'What a difference from our previous caravan, which was a four-berth side-dinette,' says Cathy. 'We had to put away the beds every morning to give us some space during the day and then make them up again at bedtime.

'Now, there's none of that. The kids have two fantastic, permanent beds; and because they're up against the rear wall, they use up hardly any space. They each have their own little window and little light, with an open shelf for all their things – and they absolutely love it.

'Because we don't need the side-dinette for beds, it gives the kids somewhere else to sit, and that table comes in useful for serving up food as well – it's right opposite the kitchen.

'It's turned out to be a brilliant choice for us.'

Pros

▶ As well as being a highly appealing four-berth option, it makes sense for five, too – the fifth bed being the lower-level one in the side-dinette. There's no need to bring the fold-out, overhead bunk into use. If you wish, this can be dismantled and left at home to save some weight.

Cons

▶ If you're touring with a complement of five or six, you may bemoan the lack of realistic kitchen workspace when preparing and serving up meals.

Remember this

An interesting alternative to the six-berth is the layout that features three fixed bunks, one on top of the other. How so? Simple – the bottom bed is right at floor level.

It's a seemingly clever use of space, but mainstream UK manufacturers have now dropped this layout from their ranges due to poor sales. Feedback from would-be customers and those who actually bought one to a large extent supports my own opinion: the bunks are all extremely compact and very quickly become uncomfortable for fast-growing children. You'll still find many triple-bunk caravans on the used forecourts – do get the family to try out the bunks before deciding to buy one.

Which side are you on?

If you walk around a caravan showroom or exhibition, you'll come across models with kitchens set against either wall. Does it matter which side it's on?

If you intend to use the awning a lot, bear in mind that the fridge exhaust vent generates a lot of heat, especially in the summer. Many caravanners therefore prefer to have the kitchen situated on the opposite wall from the entrance door for this reason. Just to complicate matters, however, some caravan fridges are on the opposite side from the rest of the kitchen.

Also, if you wish to have the kitchen window open to let steam and cooking smells escape, whoever is sitting under the awning at the time would no doubt rather they were escaping away from them!

Focus points

The main points to remember from this chapter are:

* Spend a lot of time working out which layout suits you best: it's one of the most important things to get right.

* Don't limit your search to two-berth caravans for two people, three-berth caravans for three ... and so on.

* Bowled over by an L-shape front lounge? Think very carefully – this configuration can be too compromised.

* A big end-washroom always looks impressive – but it takes up a lot of valuable space.

* A permanent-bed caravan (whether with one double bed or two singles) works best as a two-berth.

* Some permanent-bed caravans have smaller than usual front lounges. Be sure you can live with this.

* The five-berth twin-dinette layout has two distinct living/sleeping areas – good for giving kids their own space...

* ... but fixed bunks along the rear wall provide great beds and free up a lot of space.

* A six-berth caravan with fixed rear bunks is an effective layout for a family of four.

* You may prefer a caravan with an offside kitchen if you intend spending a lot of time under the awning.

4

Watch your weight – the art and science of outfit matching

In this chapter, you will learn:

- ▶ *how to work out if your car is a good match for the caravan – and vice versa*
- ▶ *the importance of noseweight*
- ▶ *what makes a great towcar.*

This chapter actually needs only a couple of sentences:

▶ Make sure your car has a powerful, torquey engine.

▶ Don't tow a caravan that (when laden) weighs any more than 85 per cent of the kerbweight of the car (i.e. the empty weight, as defined by the maker).

If life is so frantic that you only ever get around to reading the first paragraphs of book chapters, you'll probably get by just by heeding that advice alone.

The percentage game

This won't be the first time you'll come across the so-called 85 per cent 'rule'. It's not a rule, it's a guideline – but it's pretty much followed by all responsible parties involved in the business of selling caravans or doling out advice on what does or does not constitute a good outfit match.

What it sets out to achieve is to all but eliminate the risk of the caravan becoming unstable under tow; to ensure that you can motor up steep hills without having to resort to first gear and a fiendishly screaming engine; and to allow you to go about your towing business in safety and comfort, while not being a mobile barrier to the traffic following behind you. Play the percentage game and you should be able to cruise easily at the UK legal speed limits for towing a caravan, i.e. 50 mph on single-carriageway roads, and 60 mph on motorways and dual carriageways (see Chapter 10 for speed limits in the main touring destinations on the continent).

So, is that the be-all and end-all, then? If a caravan, all packed with your holiday essentials, tips the scales at 87 per cent of your car's kerbweight, should you dismiss it as an unsuitable match?

Not at all. Remember, 85 per cent is a guideline and 87 per cent is near enough for it to be perfectly acceptable. It does mean, though, that you'll have to think carefully before adding any more to the caravan's payload – don't forget we're talking about the actual laden weight of your caravan here.

If you've decided that you want to start taking the family's bikes with you, for example, or buy a bigger, heavier awning or pack a microwave in the caravan, you'll have to think about what you can take out to accommodate the new additions and keep the payload about the same.

The 85 per cent guideline is, for the most part, aimed at inexperienced caravanners. So as you gain in confidence and experience, you can think in terms of towing with a laden caravan that's getting on towards 90 per cent of the weight of the car. But as we're concerned with newcomers here, that's for another time and place.

Remember this

Weights and limits are always going to be important considerations for caravanners. But while you're counting the kilograms, don't lose sight of the fact that a caravan allows you to take far more stuff with you on holiday than you've probably been used to. If you're a family of keen cyclists, for instance, a caravan makes even more sense.

Maximum towing limit

There's another extremely important vital statistic to take into account, though – and this one carries more clout even than the 85 per cent guideline. By whatever means, you must find out what your car's stated maximum towing limit is. You'll find this in the specification charts of the car owner's handbook. If this is missing, ask your nearest dealer of the marque in question or contact the manufacturer's customer service department.

In most cases, a vehicle's maximum towing limit will be higher than the 85 per cent of kerbweight figure, in which case there's no problem – simply stick to 85 per cent. Sometimes, you'll find that the maximum towing limit is higher even than 100 per cent of kerbweight: don't even think about it. With that 15 per cent or so weight advantage in favour of the vehicle you're in control of, you'll always have the upper hand.

Pulling a caravan that's heavier than your car means that if any instability should set in – no matter how slight – it's the caravan that'll take control and momentum will gather quickly to the stage where you have a bit of a problem on your hands. Think of it as the tail wagging the dog, and you'll quickly gain a mental image of the likely scenario. Not recommended.

In some instances, the vehicle's maximum towing limit will be lower than 85 per cent of kerbweight. Then, you're bound to take heed of this lower figure, however daft it might seem. (A few years ago, a potentially superb towcar was denied a class win in the important Caravan Club Towcar of the Year competition because it was found that its maximum towing limit didn't even reach 85 per cent of kerbweight.)

You must comply with a maximum towing weight. If, in the aftermath of an accident, an insurance assessor uncovered the fact that you were towing beyond the car manufacturer's limit, you could wave goodbye to any sort of insurance settlement – they would refuse to pay out, simple as that.

Noseweight

Your car owner's handbook is also the place where you'll find the last of our trilogy of vital statistics – the car's maximum noseweight limit. In other words, it's the maximum permissible weight that can be borne by the tow hitch. This is another factor in establishing an outfit that's safe, steady and swift on the road.

Noseweight is, generally speaking, a desirable attribute. The downforce that results when the car and caravan outfit is on the move plays a valuable role in overall stability. In approximate terms, a family saloon or hatchback will more than likely have a maximum noseweight figure of between 60 and 75 kg, a larger estate car might have an 80 kg limit, and an SUV's limit will typically be between 90 and 140 kg.

So, what should you be trying to achieve? You should aim for the formula put forward by the Caravan Club: a noseweight figure of about 7 per cent of the actual weight of the caravan is the optimum for poise and stability under tow. That's in an ideal world. Remember, 'actual weight' means the weight of the caravan as you have loaded it, not any figure you'll find in a handbook.

However, as with your car manufacturer's maximum towing limit, you must adhere to the same maker's maximum noseweight limit. For the sake of example, let's say the limit is 75 kg – a common figure. If you want that to be 7 per cent of what the caravan weighs, the actual laden weight of the caravan would have to be no more than 1,070 kg. We'll talk more about actual laden weights later, but even if you've only dipped your toe into the waters of caravan weights, you'll know that's not a lot. Only the very lightest models will get anywhere near that.

How do you check what the noseweight of your caravan is? Pop over to your nearest caravan accessory shop and ask for a noseweight gauge – it's not an expensive purchase, but it's an invaluable one. A few caravans have a noseweight gauge already built in to the jockey wheel mechanism.

Load up your caravan with everything you intend to take on holiday with you and tow it to a level piece of firm ground. Lower the jockey wheel, making sure the jockey wheel clamp is on good and tight. Position the noseweight gauge directly under the caravan's hitch head (which you would normally attach to the towball) and turn the jockey wheel handle so that the caravan lowers on to the top of the gauge.

When the hitch head is in secure contact with the gauge, release the jockey wheel clamp gently until it's slack enough for you to ease the jockey wheel clear of the ground. The caravan is now being supported entirely by the gauge – and the reading you can take from it is the noseweight. You'll be able to see at a glance whether or not you're within the limit set by your car's manufacturer.

HOW TO LIGHTEN YOUR CARAVAN'S NOSEWEIGHT
What if you're not within that limit? How can you lighten the load that's bearing down on the hitch head?

The bulk of the weight on the nose of the caravan is caused by whatever you've stowed in the front area of it, i.e. in the exterior locker under the front window and in the caravan itself, forward of the axle. So lower the jockey wheel so it's in contact with the ground, clamp it good and tight, move the noseweight gauge clear and wind down the corner steady legs so you can safely enter the caravan and sort things out.

▶ If you're carrying two gas cylinders in the front locker, do you really need both? If not, leave one behind. There are lighter-weight gas cylinders on the market now that are about half the weight of a traditional one – using these can make a significant contribution towards reducing noseweight. Check the difference for yourself at your nearest LPG supplier.

▶ If your mains hook-up lead is in there, bring that indoors. The bottom of the wardrobe is a good place for it.

▶ If your awning is lying on the floor so that the bulk of it is forward of the axle, slide it back a bit.

▶ The main culprit is often the spare wheel. Bring it inside and lay it flat over the axle. Don't put it directly on to the carpet or bare floor: use an old carpet offcut or some flattened cardboard boxes to protect the floor covering and make sure it can't move when you're towing.

Now take another noseweight reading. There's a fair bet it'll be substantially lower. Indeed, you may want to reinstate a bit of weight up front if it's dropped too much.

Ultimately, the noseweight reading from some caravans will still be too high for your car's upper limit, regardless of how much ballast you jettison or relocate – especially if your car has a limit towards the lower end of the scale. You may need to look at trading up to a vehicle that gives you a bit more leeway. If you're thinking of changing cars some time in the near future in any case, ascertaining the noseweight limit of any replacement should be one of the questions you need answering if you're thinking of going caravanning with it.

In summary, then, you must adhere to the car manufacturer's maximum noseweight limit. Don't exceed it. If that limit means you can establish noseweight at or around 7 per cent of the caravan's actual laden weight, do it.

Figure 4.1 A noseweight gauge is a cheap and efficient way to help you make sure your caravan's safe for the road.

One final word on the subject: if you don't have an owner's manual for your car and need to call your dealer to find out what its noseweight figure is, be prepared for the possibility of a long pause on the other end of the line, followed by: 'Sorry, you want to know the nose what?' It's not the most universally understood statistic, but be persistent; such a figure exists for every car. Some car manufacturers may refer to it as the 'maximum vertical load on the coupling point' or words to that effect.

If you can't get a sensible answer from your dealer, speak directly to your vehicle manufacturer's customer services department or, if you're a member of either the Caravan Club or the Camping and Caravanning Club, take advantage of the excellent technical information advice lines operated by both.

Remember this

Many caravans accommodate the spare wheel in an underslung cradle attached to the chassis, rather than stowing it in the front exterior locker. This is helpful in keeping noseweight down, not to mention freeing up valuable storage space when you've set up on site.

However, many caravanners report having great difficulty in releasing a cradle-held spare wheel at the side of the road when dealing with a puncture. It may therefore be a good idea to remove it when you first get the caravan and store it as suggested above – on the floor of the caravan. On site, it can be placed in the front gas locker if there's room for it or in the car boot.

How to make the perfect match

Consider this scenario: let's say that outside my house right now is a 2011 model-year Volkswagen Passat Estate 2.0 TDI, a beautiful car to drive thanks largely to its high-tech diesel 168bhp engine, which offers a pleasing blend of low-down pulling power (i.e. torque) and plenty of smooth power for motorway cruising and overtaking.

My family and I have decided that we'd like to give caravanning a try, and we reckon the Passat will be a great towcar for the job. However, we need to find out what weight of caravan it can haul comfortably and safely before we go sniffing around the caravan showrooms.

My owner's handbook tells me that the kerbweight of the car is 1,563 kg and the maximum towing weight is 1,800 kg. That's fine – I can go with the 85 per cent of kerbweight figure (after all, I've never towed before and I want to build in as big a safety margin as I can).

I find the easiest way to find a percentage of anything is to divide the number by 100 to get the 1 per cent figure, then multiply that by the number I need.

So, my car's kerbweight is 1,563 kg; 1 per cent of that is 15.63 kg. If I multiply that by 85, I get 1,328 kg, which is my car's

85 per cent of kerbweight figure – and that, ideally, is the maximum I want any caravan to weigh when I'm towing it. I'm not going to get worried about two or three extra kilos, but now I know what I'm aiming for.

There, it's not that difficult, really. But do remember – if your car's maximum towing limit is lower than the 85 per cent figure, you must go with the lower figure.

Caravan weights demystified

In days gone by, the terminology that was used to categorize the various caravan weights seemed to have its roots planted firmly in the grounds of common sense. Unladen weight and maximum laden weight are delightfully self-explanatory terms.

Now, though, you need to get used to MIRO and MTPLM, which are – respectively – what they call unladen weight and maximum laden weight these days. The figures of some imported caravans may still be quoted using the old-style figures, but they amount to the same thing.

▶ MIRO

This stands for 'mass in running order'. That's the weight of the caravan as it rolls off the production line, plus a few essential add-ons. So if a particular caravan has a MIRO of 1,328 kg, our VW Passat estate can tow it easily. That weight is bang on the car's 85 per cent of kerbweight figure. Mind you, what good is that? If I put so much as a spare wheel, an awning and a crate of beer in it, the caravan is already starting to look too heavy for the car.

That's an easy way of ruling any caravan out of contention. If the MIRO figure is close to your car's 85 per cent figure, forget it – unless you intend to go on holiday with nothing more than your toothbrushes and credit cards.

▶ MTPLM

This is the short way of saying 'maximum technically permissible laden mass'. That's the most the caravan can weigh, fully laden and ready for the road. You must never exceed this figure.

▶ Payloads

If you subtract MIRO from MTPLM, you'll get the maximum payload for the caravan – but it's not as simple as just adding up the weight of all your goods and chattels and making sure that figure isn't breached.

Firstly, let's deal with all caravans up to and including those produced in the 2010 model year. From the payload figure, the caravan manufacturer has set aside an amount to accommodate what's known as essential habitation equipment, e.g. gas bottle and battery. The remaining amount is what's available to you for personal belongings, which itself is divided between personal effects (clothing, food, toys, bikes, awning, lager) and optional equipment. This last allowance is to take account of any extras you may specify, either at the time of ordering your caravan or subsequently from the dealer. This would include such items as an air-conditioning unit or a microwave oven, the weights for which will be listed in the caravan manufacturer's specification sheet.

Now let's consider caravans produced in the UK from the 2011 model year (in effect, this means those built from June 2010). To comply with new EU Type Approval regulations, caravan manufacturers have had to change the way they calculate a caravan's MIRO. This figure must now include an allowance for gas bottle and water (fresh-water tank, if fitted, plus some for the toilet flushing tank), which previously had to be deducted from the total user payload.

You're forgiven if all that seems slightly confusing – but to a large extent it's just shifting around some of the pieces in the same puzzle. Your caravan handbook, or the published specification sheet in the manufacturer's brochure (or on its website), will state the allocation. Ultimately, though, you need only make sure that the caravan you're towing is within its MTPLM.

Remember this

Hopefully, your caravan will come with a spare wheel and tyre. But it may not – and you can't really go caravanning without a spare wheel, can you? So, you have to factor in the extra weight of this (plus a jack and wheel brace) when doing your calculations.

▶ Weighing it all up

- ▶ If you want to be absolutely certain of the accumulated weight of everything you're taking, weigh each item on the bathroom scales before you take it on board.

- ▶ If you already own the caravan, you can load it up as if you were going away on holiday and tow it off to the nearest public weighbridge for a definitive, no-arguments reading of its actual laden weight. If the print-out tells you you're about 85 per cent of kerbweight (or within the car manufacturer's maximum towing limit, if this is lower), you can allow yourself a smug smile. Not sure where your nearest public weighbridge is? Speak to your local council.

- ▶ If you haven't yet taken the plunge and bought your caravan, the best way to assess whether or not a model on your shortlist will have enough of a payload for you and your family's needs is to allow about 100 kg for personal effects for two people and then 25 kg for each additional person. So, a family of four will need a personal payload of about 150 kg, but it's always better to allow a bit of leeway – a personal allowance of 175 kg would be just about perfect for a family of four. You should find it straightforward to find a caravan that has the capacity you need.

If all this sounds like an awful lot of fuss to go to, it's well worth the effort; and if you record the weight of individual items for future reference, it's a task you will only have to do once.

To put it in perspective, if you decide to buy the brown pair of shoes and realize the first time you wear them that they look dreadful and you should have gone for the black ones after all, you won't have any sleepless nights over your mistake. But if you go ahead without having done your research and buy that caravan because you've been told it's a today-only killer price (and the salesman has assured you nonchalantly that your car will tow it just fine), you may regret it long and hard. However unbelievable it may seem, some caravanners actually wait until they've ordered their new tourer before checking whether or not it's a good match for their car. Don't be one of them.

So, do you need to change your car?

If you've done your homework and come to the conclusion that your car would be capable only of towing a caravan that's too small for your needs, you'll need to invest in a vehicle with the necessary torque and horsepower under the bonnet and which is sufficiently heavy.

Let's destroy one myth straight away. You don't need to fall into the arms of a big 4 × 4 such as a Land Rover Discovery or Toyota Landcruiser – excellent towcars though they are – unless you're buying one of the very heaviest twin-axle caravans that do need the muscle of these big vehicles.

If you need to go 'big', my recommended first option would be to consider a good estate car or large saloon with a refined, powerful diesel engine – assuming, of course, that all the weight figures we've discussed above add up. Not only will the performance be significantly better than that of all but a select few 4x4s, but the fuel consumption will be lower.

You also need to think about those occasions when you're not towing (which, for nearly everybody, is most of the time). A 'normal' car steers and handles far better than a slab-like 4 × 4, and it's easier both to park and manoeuvre in tight spaces.

Of course, a 4 × 4 has the added benefit of a four-wheel-drive system, which will come in handy if you're attempting to pull a caravan off a wet, grassy pitch or up a muddy slope out of a rally field in winter, and the bigger ones have that see-over-hedges driving position, which is always a nice attribute when you're touring around. Some 'normal' cars, such as all Subaru models and some Audis, Volvos and Jaguars, also have all-wheel-drive transmissions for improved traction in wet, greasy or icy conditions.

If you do decide to go for a 4 × 4 for the first time, you should take advantage of one of the many training courses available that allow you to see just what an SUV-styled, four-wheel-drive vehicle is capable of off-road. Even if you would rather self-flagellate than drive your shiny, new 4 × 4 off-road, completing such a course will empower you to use that advanced transmission system to its best effect should you ever need to call on it for real.

The site of a big international caravan rally in Germany a few years ago was transformed into a chaotic quagmire of epic proportions by a huge storm. Many of the outfits that got bogged down were 4 × 4s, whose owners faced the prospect of engaging their low-ratio four-wheel drive for the first time ever. Had they been able to display the necessary finesse, they'd have picked their way clear of the maelstrom with ease instead of digging themselves into even deeper holes than those struggling with two-wheel-drive cars.

Unless you're looking to buy an especially lightweight 'micro' caravan, such as an Adria Action or the aforementioned Freedom, a very general guide is to think of a 1.8-litre petrol or 2.0-litre diesel car as the starting point for a recommended towing vehicle.

DIESEL – IT 'S ALL TORQUE

I have mentioned that my towcar of choice would be a diesel. I would have said exactly the same thing 15 years ago, when a new generation of turbodiesel-engined cars proved that you could have fun driving, while at the same time enjoying decent refinement and very good fuel economy.

Nowadays, I give that advice even more emphatically than ever. Such is the refinement when driving, it's sometimes difficult to tell a diesel engine apart from a petrol one. Performance is at a level we could only have dreamed of just a few years ago, service intervals are significantly further apart than they used to be and diesels still enjoy a considerable miles-per-gallon advantage over the equivalent petrol-engined cars.

If you're towing a caravan, there's even more reason to go diesel: torque. This measures the ability of any given engine to pull. And the more pulling power it has, the better. When you need to make a hill-start get-away with a car and caravan, it's plenty of low-down torque that will give you that shove-in-the-back helping hand. Because diesels offer their maximum torque capability at much lower revs than petrol engines, this makes towing much easier.

They have more torque, too. A diesel Mercedes 200 CDI Blue Efficiency Executive SE estate puts out 265 lb ft of torque between 1,600 and 2,600 rpm. Compare that to the petrol-engined 180 version, which offers a much more modest 184 lb ft of pulling power. That's a huge difference on paper that would translate to an equally huge difference on the road.

All this is not to say that petrol-engined cars make poor towing vehicles – I've enjoyed towing with scores of excellent petrol-powered towcars. And, when all's said and done, if you're going to use the caravan for no more than a handful of trips a year, you may be perfectly happy to take the higher fuel costs on the chin.

Remember this

One way of reducing the running costs of a petrol-engined vehicle is to have it converted to run on LPG (liquefied petroleum gas, also known as Autogas in the UK). Although a professional conversion will cost about £1,500–£2,000, you'll be on the road to recouping the outlay the first time you fill up: at the time of writing, Autogas is about half the cost of petrol. It's a cleaner fuel than petrol or diesel, so it attracts less tax.

Your car will be able to run on either gas or petrol, so you won't be left high and dry if you need to refuel and there's no Autogas outlet nearby. The difference in performance is so negligible, it's impossible to tell – it certainly won't affect towing ability in any way.

MANUAL OR AUTOMATIC?

The straightforward answer: automatic. After all, it's one less thing to do – and if you combine a sweet automatic gearbox with an electronic parking brake that engages and releases automatically, as featured on many modern cars, there's nothing much left for you to do except turn up and steer.

That advice is very firmly predicated on the automatic gearbox being a good one: a twitchy, over-sensitive auto that, with a caravan on the back, continually hunts up and down the gearbox will soon drive you mad, not to mention send your fuel bills soaring. If it behaves itself really well when solo, chances are it won't give you too much trouble when hitched up.

The only time you may feel you want to override the automatic function is when you're towing up a steep hill – and down the other side. You may want to lock into a lower gear to keep the revs spinning more freely when climbing with your heavy outfit, and to provide increased engine braking capability when descending.

Even the most basic automatic transmissions offer this facility, while an increasing number have a semi-automatic function, where you simply flick the gear lever to take control of clutch-free gear-changing yourself. You don't get rid of Big Brother completely, mind; the gearbox will still intervene and override your control if you try to set off from traffic lights in fifth gear.

If you feel happier being in full control, then a good manual transmission will serve you just as well as an automatic. There's only the slight risk of increased clutch wear if you do a lot of hill starts when hitched up, but this is likely only with lesser-powered cars that probably shouldn't be towing a caravan in the first place.

Remember this

The electronic parking brake we've just discussed – especially the type that disengages automatically as soon as you drive off – is a good friend of the caravanner, in that it allows you to pull away with both hands on the steering wheel, knowing that the parking brake will release at precisely the right moment. As well as that, it liberates space in the area where the bulky handbrake lever would normally be.

Do you need to take another driving test?

You may need to, depending on when you passed your test and what size of outfit you intend towing with. It almost goes without saying that you need a full driving licence before you're allowed to tow any trailer, so no sneaking in some towing practice on L-plates while waiting to pass your test.

Here's how the law stands on this important issue.

▶ **If you passed your test before 1 January 1997:** you have so-called category B plus E entitlement, which means you're entitled to tow any vehicle and trailer combination, as long as the vehicle's MAM ('maximum authorized mass', which is the EU technocrats' latest terminology for 'maximum gross weight' and is the same as MTPLM) doesn't exceed 7,500 kg and the combined MAM of the vehicle and trailer doesn't exceed 8,250 kg. Additionally, you must ensure that the MAM (MTPLM) of the trailer doesn't exceed the unladen weight of the towing vehicle.

In caravanning terms, that leaves the way clear to tow the biggest caravans, as long as the weight criterion in the previous sentence is met.

▶ **If you passed your test on or after 1 January 1997:** the limits are significantly lower, but still relaxed enough for you to take to the roads with a vast range of cars and caravans. Your towing vehicle must have a MAM of 3,500 kg or lower. Once again, the MAM (MTPLM) of the caravan mustn't exceed the unladen weight of the car; and this time, the combined MAM of car and caravan must be 3,500 kg or lower.

The very biggest outfits, such as a Land Rover Discovery 4 TDV6 towing a huge, twin-axle caravan, would bust that combined MAM figure by some margin, meaning that you would need to sit an additional test to have category E entitlement on your licence.

Whatever category of driving licence you hold, the full 'weight' of the law will be brought to bear on you if you exceed your car's maximum train weight (MTW). This is the legally enforceable, maximum combined weight of the car and caravan (or, indeed, any trailer).

Focus points

The main points to remember from this chapter are:

* Make life easy for yourself: try to ensure that your laden caravan weighs about 85 per cent of your car's kerbweight.
* Can't get any lower than 86 or 87 per cent? That's fine – it's a guideline. You simply want to get as close to it as possible.
* Very rarely, a car's maximum towing limit will be lower than that 85 per cent figure. If so, you must stick to the lower figure.
* Get to know the weight terminology: MIRO = unladen caravan; MTPLM = caravan's maximum laden weight.
* Know your car's maximum noseweight figure and adhere to it.
* Noseweight is good – but not too much of it. Load your caravan sensibly to keep it in check.
* A family of four should allow for a total payload of about 150 kg for personal possessions.
* In general, diesels make better towcars than petrol-engined vehicles because of the relatively greater amount of torque (pulling power) they offer. Fuel consumption is lower too – often considerably so.
* Manual or automatic gearbox? Either is good, automatic maybe a bit better.
* Don't buy the caravan first, then set about calculating your car's suitability to tow it. Sounds too obvious? People do it.

5

Ready for the road – towing made easy

In this chapter, you will learn:

▶ *about safe, effective loading of the caravan prior to setting off*

▶ *how to adapt your driving style to towing a caravan*

▶ *how to avoid instability – and what to do if it should set in.*

Like so many other things, the prospect of towing can seem a bit daunting if you've never done it before. However, like so many other things, it is anything but daunting once you've actually undertaken your first 'mission'.

In reality, the main thing to watch out for once you've been towing happily for a while is actually remembering that you are towing a caravan. If you've heeded all the advice elsewhere in this book and set yourself up with a beautifully matched car and caravan, it's all too easy to purr along the motorway, listening to the afternoon play on the radio, and forget about the big, white house on wheels following faithfully along behind you.

These lapses tend to last only as long as you avoid looking in any of your car's mirrors, which is just as well, really.

I take great pleasure in adapting my driving style to suit whatever vehicle I'm behind the wheel of. I don't claim to be a significantly better driver than anybody else – but if everyone else took that attitude, the roads would certainly be much happier, safer places to be.

So, when towing a caravan:

► think about the extra length (added consideration when pulling out of junctions; keeping side roads clear in queueing traffic, taking a wider arc when turning left)

► be aware of the added width (letting oncoming traffic pass before passing parked vehicles; avoiding especially narrow lanes)

► take account of the weight of the laden caravan (increasing the distance from the vehicle in front to allow for comfortable braking if needed; using the gearbox to avoid labouring the engine)

► show consideration for following traffic (pulling over into a lay-by or a garage forecourt to let them pass when there's a clear road in front of you and it's difficult for them to overtake).

Not only will you get a lot of satisfaction from driving a car/caravan combination in this manner, but it adds precisely nothing to a journey time.

Towing well – and the preparation that goes with doing so – will quickly become an enjoyable part of your new caravanning lifestyle. This chapter will give you all the guidance you need to achieve that.

Remember this

Considerate use of your indicators is the mark of a good driver, regardless of what you're driving – but it's an especially good habit to nurture when you're towing your caravan. Let following drivers know your intentions in plenty of time, so they can give you the space you need. This is a particularly good idea when turning right on a busy roundabout, which may involve you straddling lanes as you complete the manoeuvre.

Choosing a towbar

If your intended towcar already has one fitted, that's great. If not, you have a number of choices when it comes to deciding what to go for.

Just a word about the terminology: the towbar consists of the entire structure fitted to the underside of the towcar; the part that joins the caravan or other trailer to the towcar is the towball.

There are three types to consider.

1 Towbar with a removable towball. This slots securely into place when needed and can be quickly detached and stowed away (most usually in the spare-wheel well under the boot) when you're not towing. Towballs aren't exactly the most gorgeous things ever invented and if you want to maintain the clean lines of your car, a removable ball makes a lot of sense. You may find that you do not have any choice in the matter if a towball obscures any part of your car's number plate when fitted. If this is the case you must fit a removable one.

2 Towbar with a bolt-on towball. These are robust and cheap, and the towball is attached to a face plate by high-tensile bolts. This type is a good choice if you intend to fit a towball-mounted cycle carrier when you're not towing.

3 Swan-neck towbar. This is a one-piece item, comprising a towbar with integral towball. It looks less intrusive on a vehicle than the basic bolt-on type.

All towbars fitted to cars registered after 1 September 1998 are subject to Type Approval. This is no bad thing, as the requirement to adhere to these stringent set standards all but eliminates the risk of having an inferior product or having one that's unsuitable for your vehicle.

If you're ordering a brand-new car, you can ask for a towbar to be fitted when finalizing the specification – but do enquire about the cost first. Some car manufacturers' approved towbars are reasonably priced, but others will make you wince before you decide very quickly to fit a much cheaper aftermarket towbar – which is, in any case, subject by law to the same specification as every other one.

Most caravanners' towcars have two electrical sockets adjacent to the towball – one black and the other grey or white. The black socket is known as the 12N (i.e. 12-volt Normal) and is a universal connection point for all trailers. When you connect the black-coloured socket from the caravan to the 12N socket on the vehicle, this operates the essentials: indicators, road lights, brake lights and fog lamp.

The white or grey socket is the 12S (i.e. 12-volt Supplementary) socket. When this is connected, it allows you to operate the caravan fridge – making sure its control dial is turned to the 12-volt setting – from the car's battery when under tow. This socket also operates the caravan's reversing light(s), if fitted, and interior equipment such as lighting.

Please note: the 12-volt setting on the fridge control dial or switch does not mean you can operate the fridge from the caravan's on-board battery when you're not connected to the site's electricity supply. On this setting, it works only from the towcar's battery.

It's worth having the 12S socket for the fridge-operating function alone. Caravan fridges are notoriously slow to crank themselves up (or should that be down?) to optimum operating temperature so, if you have a journey of any length to make before you reach your chosen site, you'll be doing yourself a big favour if you want the white wine to be anywhere near drinkable that evening …

As well as that, you also have a working fridge to take advantage of during your journey – and how many motorists can claim that? Your drinks will be lovely and cool at your picnic stops, and any perishables you've picked up while shopping en route will still be edible at your journey's end.

Do remember, though, that the relay wired into this socket will prevent current flowing to the fridge when the engine is turned off, in order to make sure the car battery doesn't go flat. So, if you have a long ferry crossing, for example, either take that runny blue cheese on board with you to have for lunch or wrap it in acres of newspaper. Otherwise, prepare to suffer the awful consequences the next time you open the caravan fridge door.

If you buy an overseas-manufactured caravan – or any caravan made in the UK from September 2008 – it'll have a single, 13-pin socket instead of the familiar 12N and 12S seven-pin connectors. That's not a problem; you just need the appropriate adaptor, which every caravan accessory shop sells, if there's not one provided. Of course, if you're having a new towbar fitted you can specify a single, 13-pin socket for your car, too.

Remember this

The arrival of single electrical sockets is a welcome development. It's much less fiddly to make just the one connection, and it promises to be a more robust, reliable fitment than the previous arrangement.

Towing mirrors

By law, caravanners must have adequate rear vision when towing. The precise regulations vary from country to country, but best practice is to fit two additional mirrors. The most common means of attachment is to the car's existing door mirror, although there are types that fit directly on to the vehicle's door or front wing.

- The basic clip-on towing mirror is the most popular choice, and with good reason. They're very cheap to buy, simple and quick to fit, and work very well with most vehicles. These mirrors are attached to a pair of arms, with hooks that fit between the car door mirror housing and the glass. Two straps run around the back of the car mirror, which you tighten to ensure a snug, secure fit.

- The swivel-arm type works on a similar principle. The mirror swivels on the end of a metal tube that is attached to the top of the car door mirror housing and also includes a securing strap that reaches around the back of the housing. Because there's only the one bar, this type is a good choice for vehicles with especially large door mirrors that a basic clip-on may struggle to attach to.

- Door- and wing-mounted mirrors are rigidly mounted, meaning there's little or no movement. It's up to you to decide whether this attribute makes it worth putting up with the considerable extra bulk that makes them awkward to store when they're not in use – you should never drive a solo car with towing mirrors still attached. In the case of wing-mounted mirrors, it's also worth bearing in mind that they can't be adjusted from the driver's seat and/or passenger seat, unlike the other types.

Key point

Always carry a spare towing mirror when you go caravanning. If one is irreparably damaged on a journey or dropped and broken while you're fitting it, you'll be very glad you have that spare to hand.

A place for everything – loading explained

One of the great beauties of a caravan holiday is the sheer amount of kit you can take with you. But there are limits, of course.

In Chapter 4, we discussed at length the need to make sure you keep within all the necessary maximum weight figures. But the majority of caravans are at least fairly generous in the amount of loading margin on offer; some put more at your disposal than you will ever actually need.

Most caravans have a variety of stowage locations. Here, we're interested only in how you use these locations when you're on the move, because there are fundamental safety considerations to bear in mind. When you're set up on site, you have a free rein to put as much stuff as you like where you like.

▶ Fundamental principle no 1: When loading a caravan safely, heavy items (tins of food, barbecue, toolbox, bikes) should be at floor level, and the heaviest of all (awning, packed holdalls) should be placed directly over the axle.

▶ Fundamental principle no 2: Realize that, if you can move something around after you've stowed it, it will move around with greater alacrity when you're actually towing.

Key point

The heavy-duty carrier bags sold by most supermarkets are a caravanner's best friend. They're voluminous and near-indestructible and, because they can be used time and time again, they're very good for the environment. Use them to pack foodstuffs, kitchen utensils, toys and the like. And, while on holiday, use them to do what they do best – carry your shopping. Don't be totally without plastic carrier bags, though; they're ideal for use as bin liners.

Have uppermost in your thoughts a strategy for loading the caravan with the goal of optimum stability when towing. The lowest-possible centre of gravity is what you're striving to achieve, so your aim should be to concentrate the majority of the weight over the axle at floor level, or as near to floor level as possible. Keep heavier items away from the front of the caravan, even if they are on the floor. As well as possibly increasing noseweight to an intolerable level, all that weight bearing down on the towball will compress the car's rear suspension and compromise its handling.

This is one of the most abused loading 'rules'. Have a walk along a queue of caravans waiting to board a cross-Channel ferry, for example, and you'll almost certainly come across several culprits with easy-to-spot, poorly loaded caravans.

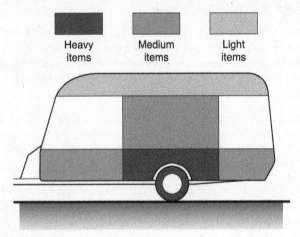

Figure 5.1 Sensible loading: How to apportion it.

Don't become one of them. When you've loaded the caravan, use your noseweight gauge to check all is well (remember, it's your vehicle manufacturer's maximum limit you must adhere to). As a final confirmation, attach the caravan to the car, walk away and take a good look at your outfit in profile. Ideally, the caravan should be sitting level, or with a very slight downward attitude.

If not, lighten the load on the front of the caravan by rearranging some of the items you've packed and you'll quickly notice the difference when you take another look.

► Bear in mind that you may want to ensure that you can access the washroom en route without having to unload and reload a mountain of stuff; the same goes for the fridge. Anything else you may need during the journey should be carried in the boot of the car or within easy reach of the caravan door.

► Bulky but fairly lightweight items, such as pillows, duvets, sleeping bags, blankets and towels should be stowed in the bed lockers, i.e. the space under the sofas or single seats.

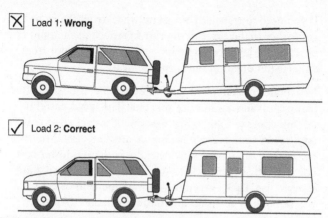

Load 1: **Wrong**

Load 2: **Correct**

Figure 5.2 The heaviest items must be over the axle.

You can then wedge in a couple of bags or boxes, using the bedding to hold them securely in place. Make sure any such bags or boxes are positioned as near as possible to the axle; don't put them too near the front – or rear – of the caravan.

▶ The best place to store your awning is on the caravan floor – right over the axle, for optimum weight distribution.

▶ If you intend to carry the family's bikes in the caravan, they should go over the axle too. Make sure they're firmly secured, so that they can't move about and cause damage. Get hold of a big roll of bubble wrap and use pieces of it to place over handlebars, pedals or any other part of the bikes that may knock against furniture during the journey. Secure the bubble wrap with rubber bands if you need to. It's great stuff for protecting the bikes' paintwork, too.

▶ By all means put food and/or drink in the fridge, although the earlier comment about stuff moving around applies.

▶ Water is really heavy, so best practice is to make sure the water heater tank is drained fully before you tow; likewise the inboard fresh-water tank, if your caravan is so equipped. There's no harm in having a small amount (a couple of litres or so) in the toilet header tank to use for flushing, just in case you need to avail yourself of what can be a very useful facility to have at your disposal!

▶ If you need to transfer your spare wheel from the front gas locker to the caravan interior to reduce the amount of noseweight, lay it on something to protect the floor from damage (an offcut of old carpet is ideal).

▶ Melamine crockery, nigh on indestructible, is favoured by many caravanners. But not this one. The word 'tasteful' doesn't come to mind when describing the range of patterns on offer in your average melamine crockery sets. You could use normal household sets instead – perhaps a lower-cost one from the supermarket – which, in any case, are much nicer to use. Pack everything with a modicum of care and you're unlikely to suffer any more breakages than you would at home.

▶ Be very wary of any packets that have already been opened, as the contents have an unhappy knack of emptying themselves during transit. Either secure them with tightly fitting elastic bands or tie them up in plastic bags. Do both if you're of an especially cautious disposition.

▶ More than once elsewhere in this book, I've mentioned the importance of stopping to check that all's well with the outfit soon after you start your journey. Part of this check (at a fuel stop, a coffee break or a quick once-over in a lay-by) should include opening the caravan door to make sure everything you've loaded inside is still snugly secure.

▶ The most forgotten-about potential nuisance? It's the loo roll in the washroom, which has a habit of unravelling itself as the miles pass by. Remove it from its holder and place it in the washroom cupboard, or slip an elastic band over it.

Remember this

Some caravans with fixed bunks along the back have an exterior-access 'garage' door on the offside rear wall. The lower bunk base hinges up to provide a capacious cargo hold, into which you can load bikes, surfboards and other awkwardly shaped items. Don't overload it when towing, though – it's not a good idea to have a lot of weight this far back.

Connecting car to caravan

The type of hitch that you have on your caravan depends on the manufacturer of the vehicle. Most caravans have hitches made by Al-Ko Kober, with Winterhoff fitments favoured by one major manufacturer. Both are supremely easy to operate, with identical general principles.

Let's now take you through the process of hitching up the car to the caravan. It's very straightforward.

▶ Before you leave the caravan for the final time, move the 12-volt rocker switch (if fitted) to the 'car' position and flick the fridge's power source to 12-volt.

▶ Ready the caravan for departure: all doors and windows locked, including sunroofs and skylights; handbrake fully on. IMPORTANT: double-check that the jockey wheel clamp is tight. Only then should you raise the corner steadies fully.

▶ You can reverse the car up to the caravan hitch head by yourself, but it's easier if you have a helper to guide you.

▶ If you are doing it on your own, don't expect to make a precision manoeuvre in one go (unless you have the luxury of a car with a colour reversing camera...). Take it very slowly and get out of the car as often as you need to so you can check your position.

▶ If you have a guide, make sure you can see him or her clearly from the driver's seat and agree on set signals as you home in on your target.

▶ Unless the caravan is a heavy twin-axle beast or it's on terrain that makes it difficult to move, you should be able to move it those last few inches to get the hitch head right above the towball. If the hitch is too low, raise it slightly by turning the jockey wheel winder.

▶ If your caravan has a remote-control motorized mover fitted, try not to look too smug as you nonchalantly guide the caravan with millimetric precision to wherever in the world your car tow hitch happens to be ...

▶ Raise the hitch handle and, holding it in that raised position, begin winding the jockey wheel so that the hitch head lowers towards the towball.

▶ When the hitch makes contact with the ball, keep winding down but release the handle. You'll hear a reassuring clunk as the hitch makes its secure connection to the towball.

▶ On Al-Ko Kober hitches, the (justifiably) much-admired button on the very edge of the hitch will pop up, changing from red to green – your confirmation that you're on. On a Winterhoff hitch, an arrow on the side will point to a plus sign, indicating the same positive result. If you can't see green for go (or if that arrow's not pointing to the plus sign), raise the handle again, wind the hitch head clear of the ball and have another try. It may sound somewhat Heath Robinson, but giving the hitch a good wiggle from side to side as you lower it on often gives it the helping hand it needs to clunk home.

▶ Now connect the breakaway cable (see Figure 5.3), which has a vital job: in the (highly unlikely) event of the caravan becoming detached from the towball when on the move, this will immediately activate the caravan's handbrake. Ideally, there will be a bespoke attachment for it on the car's towbar structure, through which you should slide the entire cable and make a loop by clipping it back on itself. If there's no such attachment, you have no choice but to loop the cable around the towball itself.

▶ When attached, make sure the breakaway cable has sufficient slack to prevent it becoming taut on the move – but isn't so slack that it may drag on the ground. By law, you must always attach the breakaway cable if one is fitted – every caravan made on or after 1 October 1982 will have one.

▶ Now connect the electrical leads to the appropriate sockets on the car: black to black, grey to grey (or, if you have the newer, single socket, just twist to lock it on securely – it fits only one way). It may be easier to kneel on the ground to do this, depending on where the sockets are situated (hence Chapter 2's recommendation to have a mat handy).

Figure 5.3 A breakaway cable must be attached if there's one fitted.

Sometimes, the leads will be on the long side when connected, making them vulnerable to dragging on the road. If so, twist them gently a couple of times – in the manner of a coiled phone lead, if you like – to reduce their length. As with the breakaway cable, though, don't allow them to become taut.

▶ Next, wind the jockey wheel up as far as it will go, then loosen the jockey wheel clamp and raise the stanchion as far as the wheel will let you. Make sure the wheel itself fits snugly under the A-frame.

▶ Tighten the clamp – not quite as tight as it will go but sufficient to make sure it can't work loose on the move and cause the jockey wheel to drop to the ground.

Your final pre-flight check

With the car and caravan successfully hitched, you're almost ready to set off. However, there are some crucial checks you need to carry out first.

▶ Check that the electrical connections have been made properly. Ask your helper to confirm that indicators (announce which one you're trying first), road lights and brake lights all function as they should on the caravan.

▶ The most common problem is the wrong indicator flashing on the caravan. It's also the most easily sorted; you've probably connected the 12N (black) plug upside-down. Refit and try again.

▶ Walk all the way around the caravan to check that all the windows are securely fastened. Check that the front gas locker and exterior hatches (the battery compartment, for example) are locked. Open the door and glance up at the ceiling to make sure skylights and sunroofs are also shut properly. Lock the door – and put the key somewhere safe straight away.

▶ Check the ground around the caravan. There are two types of caravanners: those who check the ground, and those who have to keep replacing the corner steady winders that they always leave behind.

▶ Double-check that the corner steadies are wound up fully.

▶ With the car and caravan in alignment, adjust your towing mirrors so that you can see past either side of the caravan.

Remember this

You may not always have a helper to hand when you're hitching up the caravan, but you still need to check that all the lights and indicators work. Road lights and indicators are easy to check single-handed – but what do you do about the safety-critical brake lights? If you're not able to position the caravan so that you can see the lights' reflection (in a window, or on the shiny wall of another caravan, say), place something heavy such as a conveniently handy brick or a wheel brace on the brake pedal, leave the towcar and check the lights yourself.

Key point

If you want a belt-and-braces confirmation that you've made a successful connection, start winding the jockey wheel back up again. If you can see the car's rear suspension being lifted as you do so, that's your cast-iron guarantee that the caravan hitch head has a limpet-like grip of the towball and that you're safely hitched up.

Driving off: your first tow

You're bound to feel slightly apprehensive the first time you pull away in earnest with your caravan behind you. Within a few miles, though, you'll be wondering what all the fuss was about.

You'll probably be aware of a slight 'tugging' sensation as the caravan goes over bumps or undulations on the road, but this is perfectly normal; you'll soon become used to it.

There are, though, added considerations that you need to bear in mind when towing.

▶ Always remember the extra height, width, length and weight you're now in control of. Be very conscious of it when passing cyclists or stationary obstacles at the side of the road. Keep a note of the caravan's vital statistics handy in the car.

▶ When you encounter a row of parked vehicles causing an obstruction in a busy street, you must wait until there's a safe gap in the traffic before passing them.

▶ Important: watch your speed going down hills, especially on long, exposed descents like those often found on motorways. Drop a gear – two if necessary – to benefit from some engine braking. Feather your brakes only if you really need to and, on dual carriageways or motorways, keep to the inside lane. Don't begin an overtaking manoeuvre on a descent. If every caravanner in the country read this paragraph and acted on it, accidents caused by caravans becoming unstable would be virtually eliminated at a stroke.

- When overtaking or being overtaken by a large vehicle such as a lorry or coach, increase the distance between you and it as much as you can (see Figure 5.4). This reduces the 'bow wave' effect that can induce instability, although it's usually nothing more than a momentary 'shimmy'. See the section on stabilizers later in this chapter.

- Whenever it's safe to do so, pull over into a lay-by, garage forecourt or other convenient off-road area to let following traffic past if you're the cause of a queue of vehicles. Not only will this be less stressful for you, you'll also be doing a wonderful PR job for caravans! However, if your outfit has been made with due reference to this book's advice on loading and outfit matching, you should rarely be the cause of any hold-up.

- If a hill start proves difficult (the last comment applies here, too), try pulling away at an angle when it's safe to do so. This reduces the amount of effort needed to make that initial getaway.

- Remember that you'll be using substantially more fuel when towing (the amount varies depending on outfit), so don't let your fuel gauge drop so low that it becomes a problem.

- Make a wider arc when turning and don't be rushed into it; if you need to wait for traffic to clear before making the manoeuvre, do so.

- It's worth repeating: slow down when going down hills. In an automatic with semi-manual override, use that to hold the vehicle in a lower gear.

- Take a towing course. They're great fun in a relaxed atmosphere and you'll learn lots more about caravanning than just good towing practice. Both the Caravan Club and the Camping and Caravanning Club courses are recommended. See the 'Taking it further' section for contact details.

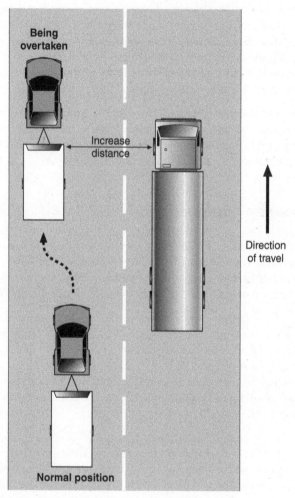

Being overtaken

Increase distance

Direction of travel

Normal position

Figure 5.4 Overtaking.

Remember this

Complacency, especially with regard to speed awareness, is something every caravanner should guard against when towing. I don't mind admitting that I've been caught out myself a few times when glancing at the speedometer at the onset of a downward slope. The combination of a well-matched outfit and a refined, quiet, modern, powerful car can dilute the sensation of speed quite markedly – so keep your eye on the speedometer. If your car has an on-board computer that allows you to set a speed at which a reminder alarm will sound, that's worth doing.

What speed to aim for when going downhill? That's hard to say, given all the factors that have to be taken into account, such as weather, wind direction, road surface and, of course, the steepness of the slope. Just take it easy, and pick up the pace again when the road levels out.

DO YOU NEED A STABILIZER?

Assuming you have a well-matched, sensibly loaded outfit and you don't speed, you'll be able to tow perfectly happily and safely without a stabilizer. Until a few years ago, when the majority of caravans began to be fitted with hitch-mounted stabilizers as standard, I had never towed with one fitted, nor had I missed not having one.

There are two types. The hitch-mounted one, which replaces the standard hitch head, is very common on new and newer caravans. It has friction pads that clamp on to the towball, which therefore needs to be kept clean and dry. You can buy this as an aftermarket option if your caravan doesn't already have it fitted.

The blade-type stabilizer attaches to a special bracket on the car and slides into another on the caravan. This needs to be stowed somewhere when not in use, unlike the hitch-type that's attached to the caravan permanently. In no way does a stabilizer compensate for a poorly loaded or overloaded caravan. Its role is to help keep things on track when there's the risk of a snake setting in.

WHAT'S A SNAKE?

You're unlikely ever to find out what this is if you follow all the rules. A snake is when the caravan becomes unstable and starts swaying from side to side, gently at first but – if not arrested – with increasing magnitude until the caravan becomes impossible to control, resulting in an accident.

Should a snake ever happen, the following strategy will bring the outfit back into line in the majority of cases.

▶ If you feel the caravan beginning to snake, lift your feet clear of all the pedals immediately. You may have heard people talk of accelerating their way out of a snake – that's the last thing you should do.

▶ Concentrate on steering the car in a straight line. The cumulative effect of the slowing vehicle and your efforts to keep it straight will gradually reduce the oscillations.

▶ Only if an accident seems inevitable should you use the brake, thus reducing the impact speed at collision. That sounds rather shocking – as indeed all road traffic accidents are – but be assured that caravan accidents are rare. Among those who have read and absorbed this chapter, they will be rarer still!

THE JOYS OF ATC AND IDC

Without a shadow of a doubt, one of the most welcome recent additions to a caravan's equipment roster is a device that works in much the same way as the electronic traction control system on many modern cars.

The main chassis manufacturers, Al-Ko (ATC – Automatic Trailer Control) and BPW (IDC – Intelligent Drive Control), offer different versions, but the way they operate and the job they do is pretty much the same. As soon as you've connected the caravan's electrics cable(s) to the car, the system is operative. The very nano-second it detects any instability from the caravan – however slight – it will automatically apply its brakes momentarily, keeping the outfit in check. Mostly, the driver will never even know this has happened.

The number of new caravans fitted with either ATC or IDC is increasing all the time. Both can be retrofitted at a cost (at the time of writing) of about £500.

Many caravanners also enjoy the peace of mind afforded by steel safety bands that, when fitted to the wheel, will prevent a blown-out tyre from dropping into the rim – which may result in dramatic instability. It also offers a brief 'run-flat' capability, allowing the stricken outfit to be driven to a safe location to effect a wheel change. Speak to your caravan dealer for more information.

Focus points

The main points to remember from this chapter are:

* Don't feel daunted at the prospect of towing – it's easy after a bit of practice.
* Choose the type of towbar carefully. You can fit a removable one to keep in the spare-wheel well when you're not towing.
* When loading your caravan, always place the heaviest items over the axle.
* Practise attaching car to caravan until it becomes a well-oiled routine.
* Always walk around the caravan/pitch to make a final 'pre-flight' check before setting off.
* Slow down when towing down hills. Excess speed on downward gradients is a major contributor to instability.
* Should the caravan start to 'snake', lift your feet off all pedals and concentrate on steering straight.
* When being overtaken by a heavy vehicle, increase the distance between it and your outfit as much as you can. Consider choosing a caravan with an electronic stability system built in, or have one retrofitted.
* Be considerate – allow following traffic to pass when it's safe and convenient to do so.
* Stop at regular intervals to check all is well with the car/caravan connection – jockey wheel still clamped tightly, no cables dragging, etc.

Love at first site – choosing a good place to stay

In this chapter, you will learn:

▶ *what different types of caravan site have to offer*

▶ *how to choose a perfect pitch*

▶ *why Certificated Locations and Certificated Sites are to be treasured.*

The only thing all caravan sites have in common is that they all cater for caravans. One may offer you the facility of a cold-water standpipe and somewhere to empty the contents of your chemical toilet – and that's it. Another one just a couple of miles away will offer you indoor and outdoor swimming pools, bars, restaurants, cabaret and crazy golf, plus satellite TV connection on your pitch. And, in between, you'll find everything else.

So, the one thing you won't be short of, after you've bought your caravan, is a choice of places to take it. There are several thousand caravan sites in the UK alone. Expand your horizons to take in continental Europe and your choice will number several hundred thousand.

Some will be indistinguishable from countless other sites; others will stand out from the crowd, for better or worse.

But – and here's a big reason why so many people swear by caravanning – when you come back to the caravan after your day out and close the door behind you, you're in the same comfortable, familiar surroundings that stay with you wherever in the world you happen to be.

Caravan sites in the UK

By sticking with the British Isles for the time being, geographically, hardly anywhere is out of bounds to you. Both the Caravan Club and the Camping and Caravanning Club have sites on their network that are within easy striking distance of London. You'll find club sites with bus-from-the-front-gate access to tourist hotspots where taking the car is a bad idea – York, Cambridge and Edinburgh, for example. Many commercial sites offer the same benefits.

At the other extreme, there are dozens of great sites spread throughout the Highlands of Scotland, one of Europe's last great wildernesses. All the country's National Parks – the Lake District, the Peaks, Dartmoor, all of them – are well catered for by caravan sites. Seaside? Spoiled for choice. Walking distance of a great pub? Some small sites are actually in the grounds of pubs.

Remember this

The surge in the popularity of caravanning in the UK means that it's even more of a good idea to book your pitch at your chosen site (or sites) as far in advance as possible. Some long-standing caravanners bemoan the fact that it's becoming increasingly hard to turn up on spec at a site and find a pitch, especially at peak times. School holidays and Bank Holidays – Easter in particular – are when the pressure is most on.

If you haven't booked in advance, I recommend phoning the site on the day itself. Not only may this save you a wasted journey, but the site warden may be able to suggest an alternative.

DECIDE WHERE YOU WANT TO VISIT

Only you know what kind of holidays or short breaks you like. Maybe you want a bit of everything: an all-singing, all-dancing two weeks with the family at a big, busy holiday park on the south coast in the summer holidays; and later in the year, with the kids packed off to the grandparents, a couple of nights away by yourselves on a farm in the Chilterns, where breakfast consists of eggs laid that morning by the hens you passed (and hopefully didn't run over) on your way in.

The first thing is to decide which area you want to visit, and to draw up a list of things you want to do when you're there. Don't want to cook? Make sure there are good places to eat within easy striking distance (within walking distance if you're looking forward to a glass or two of something nice).

DECIDE WHAT SORT OF ENVIRONMENT YOU WANT

Crave peace and quiet more than anything else? It would be best to avoid that site alongside the bypass and the main west coast railway line, then.

Get online or buy the specialist magazines to read what other caravanners have to say about the sites they've visited. Invest in a caravan site guide where all the listed sites are visited every year by the authors – that way, you can be sure you're benefiting from up-to-date information.

If you're caravanning with children, put a big tick next to any site that has a play area consisting of anything more than a couple of tired swings and a slide that's not even slidy any more. Do, though, make a mental note to avoid being pitched next to said play area – its first customers invariably arrive just after 7 a.m. and its last leave when their parents come out with torches to look for them.

Remember this

The satellite images on Google Maps (go to www.google.co.uk and click on 'Maps') can be extremely helpful in giving you a sneak preview of the environs of a site you've never been to. The site's brochure may not have mentioned anything about the M62 being on the other side of the perimeter fence, but the spy in the sky will reveal all ...

The Streetview function on Google Maps is also a useful tool: use this to check the approaches to your chosen site and to identify landmarks. It'll be helpful, for example, to know that you need to be ready to turn right immediately after the left-hand bend where that pretty, bright yellow, thatched cottage sits.

Similarly, being pitched not too far from the shower/toilet block is fine. Being pitched within hearing distance of the hand driers and the chap who whistles out of tune all through his lengthy shower is quite another.

If you're given a pitch you don't like, ask to move to another; unless the site's full, it won't be a problem. If a site's not too busy, you may be handed a site map and invited to go and choose which pitch you'd like.

CHOOSING THE TYPE OF PITCH YOU WANT

Given the choice, there are a number of factors to bear in mind:

▶ If the weather's good, a grass pitch is always nice but, if possible, try to make sure that at departure time you'll be able to hitch up to the caravan with the car's driven wheels on a grippy surface (tarmac or gravel), just in case an unexpected downpour makes the going slippery. This is obviously less of an issue if your vehicle is a four-wheel drive.

- In which direction will the caravan be facing when pitched? Do you want the sun bearing down on the front window at high noon?

- Trees are great for shade, but a nightmare when it rains. Rainwater from the foliage will be drumming down on your caravan's roof long after the shower has stopped.

- Is the pitch next to the main thoroughfare to the shower block/ reception/site shop? If it is, that's highly convenient – but there will be a lot of people to-ing and fro-ing past your front window.

- Be as choosy as you can be, and if you realize you've made a mistake in checking into a site that falls short of what you were expecting, another of the great USPs (unique selling points) of caravanning comes to the fore – you can pack up and go somewhere else.

As discussed earlier, this can be easier said than done in high season or on a Bank Holiday weekend, but always make sure you have a couple of site guides stashed away in one of your caravan's drawers (or online details saved as a favourite on your smartphone, tablet or laptop) as you should usually be able to find somewhere nice that has a vacancy for you. In this quest, it helps to be a member of the Caravan Club or the Camping and Caravanning Club, because you then have access to these organizations' Certificated Locations and Certificated Sites respectively.

CERTIFICATED WHAT?

There are thousands of Certificated Locations (CLs) and Certificated Sites (CSs) spread throughout the country – but the chances are you've never seen one. That's because, by their very nature, CLs and CSs are often tucked away out of sight in a farmer's field or in the meadow at the back of a big country house – and the only way you can stay on them is by being a member of either the Caravan Club or the Camping and Caravanning Club.

This vast network of sites – there are about 2,500 CLs and 1,500 CSs – have been given such officious-sounding names because an Act of Parliament has allowed them to exist in the first place.

In a nutshell, the landowners have been granted a certificate that allows them to use a designated area of their land for use as a CL or CS. Regardless of how big the field or paddock is, the maximum number of caravans or motorhomes that can be on site at any one time is five – although there's no limit to the number of tents.

These sites are accessible only to members of the relevant club, but you can find out where they all are by browsing each club's website. To find out the precise address of a Caravan Club CL when online, you need to log in as a member. The Camping and Caravanning Club, on the other hand, makes its CS addresses freely available.

These sites are regarded by those in the know as something of a national treasure. They crop up in quite the most unexpected places and some give you memorable views of the countryside that simply aren't available to anyone else because of their situation on private property.

Here's a devotee, painting a picture that's not untypical.

Case study

'We once stayed on a beautiful CL that we reached by driving along about a quarter-mile length of farm track, opening and closing two gates in the process, and then choosing our own pitch anywhere on a huge, manicured, hilly field. We had an amazing view of Loch Ness and the surrounding mountains we'd never had before – and which we've never forgotten since. We were charged £5 for the night, but would have paid more for such a beautiful spot. Not that I told the owner that at the time, of course.'

Tony Fitzsimmons, Leyland, Lancashire

Is there a catch? That depends on your outlook. At the very least, all the owner of a CL or CS has to provide is a fresh-water supply and a chemical waste-disposal point – often just a drain cover in a distant corner of the field. And that, indeed, is what a large number do provide, so you're reliant totally on your caravan's 12-volt electrical and gas systems as well as, of course, the on-board washroom facilities. If the idea of staying on lots of CLs/CSs appeals (quite right, too), a decently specified washroom should be suitably high on your wish list when choosing your caravan.

Furthermore, the remote, rural locations of these sites dictate that the pitches will usually be grassy and sometimes on a slope. That brings us back to the potential difficulty of hauling your outfit off site when the time comes to go home.

That may not be as big a problem as it sounds. If you're on a working farm, as many certificated campsites are, the owner's tractor or Land Rover won't be far away. I know of at least one site – there will be more – in the Peak District where the owner offers as a matter of course to use his Land Rover to tow visitors' caravans up the awkward slope to get back to terra firma.

A lot of CL/CS owners have invested heavily in their sites. Scan the listings and it's quite easy to draw up a shortlist in any given area of those that offer electric hook-ups. Some go further still by laying on showering and toilet facilities.

The increasing presence of fitted solar panels on caravans is a great boon for those owners who frequent the majority of CLs/CSs that don't offer an electric hook-up. Even a modest solar panel on the roof of a caravan will make an appreciable difference to the amount of time the battery stays charged. Some manufacturers offer this as an option on selected models, or you can have one retrofitted.

Another benefit of a solar panel is that your battery will still work even after your caravan has been laid up in storage for a while – really useful if you need to have the lights on, want to listen to the radio while cleaning inside or move the caravan via its motorized mover (if fitted).

You can stay on a CL/CS for up to 28 consecutive days so, if you do find a cracker that's in the area you want to go touring in, and which has more than just the basic facilities on offer, it can make a fabulous base for a longer holiday. Okay, perhaps they're not obvious choices if you're holidaying with children but, in my experience, they quickly come to appreciate the beautiful surroundings and the freedom to run around at will.

Remember this

The rather enthusiastic tone of what you've just read about CLs and CSs is no coincidence – I'm a huge fan. Both the clubs which oversee these sites run annual awards, the results of which are published in their respective members' magazines and websites. This will give you a steer towards some of the very best ones, although chancing across an otherwise unsung CL or CS that becomes a personal favourite is always a possibility when there are so many to choose from.

Sites for family holidays

You couldn't ask for more of a contrast to certificated campsites than the big, multi-million-pound holiday sites that are geared up for peak-season holidays, when hundreds of families arrive with their caravans within a few days of each other at the start of the school summer holidays.

Although these establishments are not the places to go in order to get away from it all – quite the opposite, in fact – the best of them are very well run, with facilities that are absolutely superb. On many, touring caravan pitches are in addition to hundreds of permanently sited caravans (most people refer to them as 'static caravans', although you may see them advertised as 'caravan holiday homes'). This means that, when full, the sites are incredibly busy.

Do your homework and find out what facilities and attractions are on offer. Otherwise you could end up paying a lot of money (they're expensive places to stay in high season) for amenities that you or your family have no intention of using.

For example, there may be nightly entertainment in the giant complex that forms the hub of the site, but which isn't really your thing. The site owners may just have invested in a million-pound daredevil roller coaster as the main attraction in the fairground section, but you suffer from vertigo and the kids are still too young for it. You'll be paying for these facilities even though you're not using them.

You can ask for a brochure to be mailed to you but all the big holiday sites now have their own websites where you can download one. As with so many things, the internet allows you to cover a lot of ground very quickly; in the space of an hour, you can ponder over your shortlisted sites, take 360-degree virtual tours, compare prices, check availability and even get everything booked.

Regardless of how many attractions the site itself has to offer, though, find out what there is to see and do in the local area. You'll need to have a change of scenery at least some of the time ...

Key point

When phoning ahead to book a site you've never been to before, ask the owners for precise directions for the last mile or so. If you take a wrong turning or don't spot the half-hidden entrance until it's too late, you may end up having to travel several more miles until you get the opportunity to make a safe turning with the outfit. As previously suggested, take a peek on Google Streetview.

FACILITIES FOR DISABLED CARAVANNERS

Many sites offer first-class access for people with physical disabilities, including dedicated shower and toilet facilities. Both the major clubs, for example, have hundreds of sites between them that cater for wheelchair users, while some – perhaps due to the nature of the terrain – are more suitable for disabled people who can walk.

Before booking a pitch, it's always best to check with the site that your specific needs will be catered for.

Caravan sites overseas

Most of the points to look out for are just as valid for continental caravan sites as they are for British-based ones – and the variety of sites available to you is every bit as diverse.

Most European countries, France and Spain included, have a nationwide network of municipal sites – each of which is run by the relevant local authority – that are generally very good. A lot of them don't take bookings and it's rare for them to be full, so they can be a good choice if you're touring around without definite plans.

When staying at overseas caravan sites, bear the following in mind:

► Always make sure you have a good supply of cash. If you're using municipal sites in France, for example, it's safer just to assume they don't accept payment by credit or debit card.

► In France in particular, you may find that the toilets in some sites supply neither loo roll nor soap, so you have to try to remember to take those with you from the caravan when you use the facilities. Don't take that as an indication that the toilets are scary places to visit, though: generally speaking, they're very clean.

► Take enough bottled gas to last the duration of your trip, as the type used in the UK requires a different connector. It's not an insurmountable problem if you do run out, however – as long as you've come prepared with an adaptor (available at most caravanning accessory shops) that will allow you to use Campingaz, which you'll find just about anywhere on the continent.

► While you're in the shop, buy a continental mains hook-up adaptor. Chances are you won't use it because most sites will have the same connectors found on British sites, but they cost just a few pounds and having one means you're covered for most eventualities. Stow it in the front gas locker and forget about it until you need it.

► One last item for your shopping list: a mains polarity tester. Although unlikely, you may connect to the mains supply of some continental sites and encounter reverse polarity – i.e. where the live and neutral feeds get their wires crossed (literally), making it unsafe to use mains appliances. Immediately on connecting to the mains, plug in your polarity tester. It will tell you straight away whether or not there's a problem (it's not one I've ever encountered personally). Disconnect and try another mains bollard, because the reverse polarity may be isolated to that one unit.

Remember this

Some sites do a roaring trade based on the fact that they're situated near popular ferry ports, including Dover, Portsmouth and Holyhead in the UK, Dun Laoghaire in Ireland, Calais and St Malo in France, and Bilbao and Santander in northern Spain. The case for using them is overwhelming: far better to spend a relaxing night with a short hop to your ferry (or Eurotunnel train) the next morning than a stress-inducing long haul that will, inevitably, take longer than you've planned for.

Site rules

Poorly enforced caravan site rules – and subsequent falling-outs with the management over demands for refunds and apologies – result in more complaints and bad feeling than just about anything else in caravanning.

The main point of contention is usually contravention of a night-time curfew, which the majority of caravan sites in the UK and abroad have in their rule books. Typically, it's 11 p.m., although it may be later on a few of the bigger sites in high season.

That's not to say an air-raid-warden-type employee will be doing the rounds at 11:01 p.m., shining a torch in your face and ordering you to get to bed. Guests are simply required to exercise some basic courtesy so that those who don't want to stay up as late as you do can enjoy a peaceful night's sleep unmolested by car engines, raucous outdoor drinks parties or late-night sing-songs.

Focus points

The main points to remember from this chapter are:

* There are thousands of caravan sites in the UK alone. You'll quickly get to know the type of site you like, building up a growing list of favourites as time passes.

* Membership of either of the big two caravanning clubs gives you access to the wonderful Certificated Location or Certificated Site networks.

* Make a checklist of the things you want to do while you're away: this will help you narrow down your choice of sites.

* A site with a good play area is a definite plus when caravanning with children.

* Don't accept a pitch you don't like. Ask to be moved to another.

* Always keep a couple of site guides in a caravan drawer – you may decide you want to move on somewhere else.

* Bigger holiday sites with lots of facilities can be very expensive. You'll be paying for these facilities even if you don't use them.

* Make sure you have precise directions for the site you're travelling to. Some may involve a particular detour to avoid a narrow lane or awkward turning.

* You'll find municipal caravan sites in many bigger towns and cities in most continental countries. They're usually of good quality.

* Take enough gas to last for the duration of an overseas trip – two 6kg cylinders should be more than ample for a two-week holiday.

7

Setting up on site and keeping everything running smoothly

In this chapter, you will learn:

▶ *how to pitch your caravan with the minimum of fuss*

▶ *how to connect up the services*

▶ *how to make the best use of them.*

Driving up to your pitch can be a bit daunting at first, especially if you're rolling on to a well-populated site with all your neighbours sitting outside their caravans enjoying lunch and ready to watch the new arrival – i.e. you – reverse the caravan on to what seems to you like an unreasonably tight patch of ground. Even when you have a bit of experience behind you, the simplest things take on a new difficulty when the eyes of the world are on you.

In this chapter you'll find the hints, tips and guidance you need to make your watching neighbours wish that they could make such a confident, assured arrival, not to mention having the caravan all up and running so quickly.

The arrival

The most important thing to remember when manoeuvring your caravan is that every single aspect should be carried out as slowly as possible. The slower the caravan is moving, the more time you're giving yourself to assess your progress, to make finely tuned adjustments or to stop, set it all up again and have another go.

▶ Your plan of attack should be in place before you've even left site reception. When you check in, find out if you can leave the outfit parked up while you go and recce the pitch that's been allocated to you. If you can't do that, ask how good the access is to your pitch: can you simply drive on to it or will you need to reverse?

▶ Be quite open that this is all quite new to you and that, if there's someone who can just stick around and offer a bit of help or advice while you manoeuvre the caravan into place, that would be great. You'll very quickly find that the world of caravanning is, by and large, populated by people who'll willingly make a detour to help you out. So, as a beginner, it makes an awful lot of sense to tap into that wealth of experience and goodwill.

▶ It also makes sense to have practised your caravan reversing skills before your first site visit. As mentioned in an earlier chapter, both the two big caravanning clubs in the UK offer caravan manoeuvring courses, and I can't recommend them highly enough. Not only will you come away enriched with new-found skills, you'll be in the company of skilled instructors, all with decades of caravanning and towing experience behind them, and at whom you can fire all sorts of questions all day. You'll find details of how to take a course in the 'Taking it further' section.

► Even if you do take a course, it's practice that makes you perfect. So, if you live anywhere near an industrial estate or retail park with suitably deserted car parks and roads in the evenings, hitch up and go round there. Try out lots of different scenarios – reversing in a straight line, to the right, to the left – and use markers of some kind to give you something to aim for.

► Take your time: get out, have a good look

So, let's get back to your pitch. Remember – you're not in a hurry. Before you reverse on to it (let's assume for the purposes of this illustration that's what you're doing), pull the car handbrake on, switch the engine off and get out to have a walk around the pitch. Even if you have someone with you to help guide you into place, it's still useful for you, as the driver, to know the lie of the land.

► If you're going to be putting up an awning, remember to leave enough room for it. Maybe that means positioning the offside wall of the caravan near a bordering hedge, which has some lethal-looking thorns on it. They'll leave their mark on your gleaming sidewalls if you get too close.

► And nor do you want to reverse too far back, because the mains hook-up pole may be there, for example, and you really don't want to be bumping into that.

► This bit may sound rather cheesy, but it really will help; when you've had your scout around, stand back and draw yourself a mental picture of exactly where you want the caravan to end up. Use your hands to sketch out the imaginary arc that the vehicle will form as you make the turn. Then get in and do it for real.

Reversing made easy

I like reversing a caravan; I like the sense of achievement in making it do what I intended it to do. I don't get it wrong that often – not because I'm so much better at it than anybody else, but because I probably do it more slowly than just about anyone else I've ever seen attempt it. Slower-than-walking-pace slowness, that's the secret to successful reversing.

Reversing so the caravan goes back at an angle is the most common manoeuvre, so let's focus on that.

▶ Let's imagine that you're parked on the site road and want to reverse on to the pitch, which is on the left-hand-side of the outfit and joins the road at right angles. Begin the manoeuvre with the car and caravan positioned in as straight a line as possible and move forward far enough so that you can start off by making the turn gently and tighten it up if you need to.

▶ If you have a passenger or helper watching your progress from outside the vehicle, lower the front windows so you can hear his or her guidance as well as see it.

▶ To get the caravan to begin its rearward journey in the chosen direction, you turn the steering wheel the opposite way to the one you would if you were reversing solo, i.e. without a caravan.

▶ In this example, we're reversing around to the left: so we'll start the manoeuvre with the steering wheel turned to the right. Turn the wheel gently; don't give it too much lock until you can see the angle at which the caravan is turning. If you need to make it turn just a bit more tightly, turn the steering wheel – gently – a bit more to the right, and see how the caravan's rate of turn increases.

▶ Because you're doing this at a slower speed than you've probably driven anything in your entire life before, you're building in a huge comfort margin for yourself. Even if you do have someone checking your progress from outside, get out yourself and have a look – it endows you with additional information, which is no bad thing.

▶ If you've made the turning a bit sharper than you intended, just drive forwards, straighten up and have another go, this time adding even more finesse to your control of the steering wheel.

▶ **Straightening up**

When you're happy that the caravan is creeping back at the angle you want it to, that's the time to bring the steering wheel back to steer 'with' the caravan. In other words, the steering wheel will pretty much be in the same position it would be if you were reversing solo.

Once again, though, don't over-compensate. You'll soon see for yourself that a single-axle caravan is a flighty beast that thrives on the minimum of input from you.

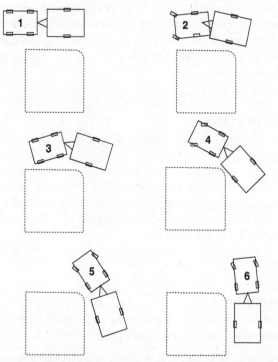

Figure 7.1 There's no substitute for practice when learning to reverse – try it as often as you can.

If you overdo this final part of the manoeuvre, you run the risk of a jack-knife situation, i.e. where the bodywork of car and caravan meet up with each other because the angle of turning is just too tight.

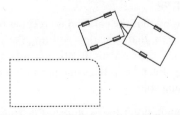

Figure 7.2 Care when reversing will eliminate the risk of a jack-knife.

Bear in mind that, unless you've been allocated an unusually tight pitch to reverse into, there's no need to achieve perfection (no harm in trying, granted). If you have one or more pairs of willing hands, all you need do is reverse it so far, uncouple and push or pull the caravan into place. Or feel very glad of your motorized mover!

Remember this

Believe it or not, reversing in a straight line probably calls for more finesse and more concentration than reversing at an angle. If you can find enough spare ground, give it a try: what you want to achieve is to keep just the merest hint of caravan sidewall visible in the driver's door mirror. Too much appearing? Ease the steering wheel accordingly. Can't see it at all? Ease it back the other way. Gently does it... It's thoroughly rewarding when you get it more or less right!

Case study

Colin Davies from Swansea recalls arriving on site during his first foreign excursion with his caravan a few years ago:

'I was being led to a lovely looking pitch on a site on the Costa Blanca, which was bordered by exotic trees and shrubs. Problem was that there was very little room for error with all that stuff about, not to mention lots of people relaxing outside their caravans, all watching me. I was still scratching my head, working out my angles, when I was almost run over by the chap from the caravan site single-handedly hauling the caravan into the ideal position. It was a lesson learned.'

Ask yourself: 'Can we push it?' If the answer's 'Yes', do it. Make life easy and save the reversing for another day. There's nothing wrong with that approach at all.

If you've used the car to get the caravan on to the pitch, though, don't be in too much of a hurry to unhitch. Have a walk around the outside of the caravan first and see if you want to make any fine-tuning adjustments. If you do, it's always going to be easier to let that nice, big internal combustion engine do all the work instead of you.

REVERSING A TWIN-AXLE CARAVAN

So far we've discussed how single-axle caravans respond best to gentle steering inputs. While that's still true of their bigger, twin-axle brethren, there's a bit more of a margin of error when reversing a four-wheel caravan. Because their imprint on the ground is that much greater, they turn much more predictably and are therefore generally easier to back into any given space than a single-axle.

Mind you, that's just as well. Once you've unhitched a twin-axle caravan from the car, you risk inducing a hernia trying to manoeuvre it by hand. If the extra living space afforded by a twin-axle appeals to you, don't hesitate to have it fitted with one of the motorized movers, of which much mention has already been made. This clever device attaches to the caravan axle and, operated by the owner using a hand-held remote control, uses the vehicle's 12-volt battery power to shift a tonne-and-a-half or more of caravan into the tiniest of spaces.

They're highly effective and can ease the caravan uphill or make it swivel on the proverbial sixpence. They're not cheap, but try finding a caravanner who owns one who doesn't think it was worth every penny.

Of course, you've got to drive to your pitch first. Some site roads, especially on overseas sites, are smaller than usual – and there's nothing like negotiating your way through a busy holiday site, with bikes, barbecues, recliners, windbreaks and other leisure paraphernalia dominating neighbouring pitches, to make an already big twin-axle caravan feel even more enormous.

The same applies if you're negotiating your way into a small, hideaway-type site that involves driving through farm gates, for example.

Key point

When booking any site you're not familiar with, ask about access with a twin-axle caravan. Over the years, I've visited a few sites where care has been required with a single-axle tourer, never mind a far bigger four-wheeler.

You're on! Now to get it on the level

If your allocated pitch is uneven to any noticeable extent, you can take steps to make sure the caravan sits as level as possible. The first step is to pay a visit, well before you go off on holiday, to your caravan accessory shop and invest in a spirit level, a couple of wheel chocks and some levelling ramps. Stick them in the front locker of your caravan or where you can get to them easily and, with a bit of luck, that may well be the last time you ever handle them. If you have a knack for choosing flat, level pitches every time you go away, they'll be forever superfluous.

But it's as well to be prepared.

▶ You can usually raise or lower the jockey wheel to ensure the caravan is sitting level front-to-back; it's side-to-side unevenness that needs a bit of help from levelling blocks. This is an important aspect to get right. Not only will it feel like you're sitting or sleeping on a hill but, if the angle of lean is anything other than insignificant, you may not be able to operate the fridge.

▶ Most accessory shops will have a variety of plastic levelling ramps and blocks on display, costing anything from about

£5 to £20. It's really just personal preference, as they're all very, very easy to use. Maybe the blocks have a slight advantage in being easier to stash away in a tight space, but that's about it.

▶ If you can see or even just suspect that the caravan is sitting higher on one side, place your spirit level horizontally somewhere suitable – on the front chest or on the A-frame just behind the handbrake, for example – and all will be revealed. No spirit level? A glass of water will do.

▶ Fetch the levelling ramp and place it squarely in front of the caravan wheel on the lower side. No levelling ramp either? See if the site shop can help you out or have a scout around for some suitably sized blocks of wood (it's surprising what you can find lying around).

▶ At crawling pace, drive forwards so that the caravan wheel eases on to the ramp. Your helper will be watching the spirit level and will let you know when it's reading dead-centre. If you're using blocks, you just put the requisite amount in place, building them up into a sort of winners' rostrum configuration.

Time to unhitch

Great – you're on and you're level. Now you can unhitch the car and park it up. Before you start uncoupling anything, though, you need to make sure that the caravan is secure. The following routine will soon become second nature but, until it does, memorize it and go through it methodically every time.

▶ Engage the car's handbrake or parking brake. Put it in first gear (or 'Park' if it's an automatic) and switch off the engine.

▶ Pull on the caravan's handbrake fully. On some caravans, you'll find that the handbrake sets itself to full-on as soon as you engage it.

▶ If you've used levelling blocks or a levelling ramp, chock the wheels at the rear.

▶ Loosen the jockey wheel clamp just enough for the wheel itself to make contact with the ground.

▶ Important: Retighten the clamp to support the jockey wheel stanchion. Remember, as soon as you unhitch from the car, this is the sole means of support for the caravan. As I write this, it's only a few weeks since I last witnessed the unfortunate consequences of not tightening this clamp sufficiently, i.e. the caravan thumping down unceremoniously on to its nose, with all the potential for damage that brings with it.

▶ Disconnect the electrical plug(s) from the sockets on the car and place neatly out of harm's way – most caravans have pre-formed receptacles on the A-frame (near the handbrake) for them to slot into.

▶ Disconnect the breakaway cable from the car and place that neatly out of harm's way as well.

▶ Lift up the hitch handle on the caravan and, supporting it like that, start winding the jockey wheel mechanism up. The hitch head will lift clear of the towball, at which point you can move the car clear.

▶ You may sometimes find that the hitch doesn't seem keen to disengage from the towball. It's likely that the hitch mechanism has become compressed as you've reversed on to the pitch. Making sure that the caravan's handbrake is on, drive the car forward very, very slightly – just enough for the hitch to de-compress. You should now be able to unhitch easily.

▶ Lower the four corner steadies to stabilize the caravan. Don't be tempted to use them as load-bearing jacks – they're not designed for that purpose.

Setting up the caravan

If you're connecting to the site's mains electricity, do this first to get the fridge operating straight away.

▶ In the interests of safety, check that the mains switch inside the caravan is in the 'off' position. Attach the mains cable to the caravan's socket first, then, uncoiling the cable as much as possible to prevent heat build-up, plug it in at the site pole.

▶ On some sites – including Caravan Club ones – you'll need to give the plug a quarter-turn clockwise after you've inserted it to make the connection. There will be a notice to this effect on the pole.

▶ Now go back inside the caravan and turn the mains switch on. And just to confirm that you're plugged in, flick your fridge power-source switch on to the mains operation position. If the confirmation light comes on, you'll know that you're in business.

▶ Now turn to the caravan's 12-volt control panel. Select the 'caravan' setting. The very fact that you're connected to the mains means that there will be no drain on your battery and, if you have an on-board battery charger, this will also give it a full charge, ready for the next time you need to rely on it.

Turn on the gas supply by turning the dial on top of the cylinder in your gas locker all the way around to the 'on' position. To confirm that gas is getting through, turn on one of the burner control knobs on the hob – you should hear the tell-tale hiss.

If you can't hear it, no gas is making it through the system, which will be for one of three reasons:

1 There isn't enough gas in the cylinder, so you'll have to exchange it for a full one or switch to a spare cylinder, if you have one.

2 The gas appliance itself isn't turned on. Every gas appliance on board will have its own individual on–off knob. Locate these (they're usually to be found at floor level inside a cupboard) before you take the caravan anywhere and familiarize yourself with how they operate. When a knob is vertical, in line with the pipe, it's open. If it's horizontal, lying at a right angle to the pipe, it's off.

3 The caravan isn't sufficiently level for the gas to make its way through the pipes – use your spirit level (or glass of water) to check it out. It may be that there's an air block in the system somewhere, in which case keep turning the dial – the gas should eventually force the air out.

You shouldn't be able to detect any smell of gas during normal operation. The makers of LPG (liquefied petroleum gas) endow it with an odour as a warning sign – if you can smell it, there may be a leak. In this case, immediately turn off the gas at the cylinder and check that all connections are sound.

Key point

After you've turned on the gas at the cylinder, get into the habit of igniting one of the rings on the gas hob (or the grill) first, before you try to turn on any other gas appliance (fridge, space heater or water heater). Because the jets are bigger on the cooker, this will help ensure a good through-put of gas and expunge any air lock in the system.

Now sort out the water system. In nearly every case, this involves connecting one end of a submersible pump to the appropriate socket on the outside wall of the caravan and dunking the other end into your (full) fresh-water container.

▶ Inside the caravan, turn the water pump switch on. The 12-volt system will spring to life, drawing in enough water from the container to fill the water heater (and the onboard water tank, if your caravan is so equipped). While this is happening, go back outside and make sure no water is cascading out from underneath the caravan. If it is, don't worry – it just means that the water heater's drain plug, attached to the unit itself, has been left open. Close it, and all should be well.

▶ If water is spurting out from where the submersible pump attaches to its socket on the caravan wall, you've not made the attachment securely. Turn off the water pump switch inside the caravan, remove the submersible from the socket and refit, making sure you've made a good connection. It's a good idea to remember the bit about switching off the pump first. If you don't, you will get a thorough drenching.

Choosing and using a caravan shower

Bear in mind that unless you're on an expensive, fully serviced pitch, where you have access to your own personal water tap with a direct connection to the caravan (buy a mains water adaptor hose from any caravan accessory outlet, if the idea of that appeals), you will have a finite supply of water at your disposal when you walk into the shower cubicle. By the time you're happy with the flow and the temperature, you'll already have gone through several litres; and the continual need to switch off the tap(s) every couple of minutes to conserve supplies will soon become tiresome.

Doing so is not a problem once in a while, though, and there will be times when you'll be very glad to be able to retreat from a shower-block queue back to the sanctuary of your caravan's delightfully queue-free shower cubicle.

Make sure that the water supply to your caravan is brim-full before you start and, conversely, that your waste-water container is nearer empty than it is full – a shower obviously uses a lot of water and can overwhelm a container that quickly runs out of spare capacity. It goes without saying that, if the container becomes full, so will the waste pipe running into it; and the water will have nowhere to go except to loiter in ever-increasing volume in the shower tray around your feet.

It's not a huge problem if you've forgotten to turn the hot water on, because a caravan's water heater is an impressively efficient performer that should give you enough hot water for a shower in 15 minutes or so. If you're in a hurry, you can make it work even more speedily by running it on gas and electricity at the same time, although not every model has a dual-fuel water heater.

Remember this

Dual-fuel capability from the caravan's water heater and space heater is the ultimate in convenience, as it obviously gives you a choice of power source – gas or mains electricity. Because you pay a flat fee for electric hook-up, you can run both of these appliances on electricity effectively free of charge. If you operate them on gas, you're running down your supply of LPG, which you'll have to replace at your own expense.

Always remember to remove the protective plastic cowl that sits over the water heater exhaust on the exterior wall before attempting to run the system on gas; otherwise it simply won't work. These cowls are notoriously stubborn beasts to remove, so don't be afraid to exert a bit of muscle power when doing so.

In Chapter 6, I advocate keenly the patronage of smaller, rural sites with not so much as a WC, never mind a shower block, so it does make sense to choose a caravan with a shower that you'd be happy to use at least occasionally. You'll see that a lot of caravans' washrooms are covered in textured wallboard – this isn't ideal if you're going to be showering more than once in a while, because its water-repelling properties are limited and may lead to problems in the future.

The separate, cylindrical shower compartment, with fully sealed lining and a sliding door enclosing it, is the most practical arrangement in this regard. Some are a bit mean in terms of their stowage provision for shower gel, shampoo and the like, which is a minor irritant, so that's another little-but-important criterion that carries some weight when you're comparing otherwise very similar caravans with each other.

A caravan with a blown-air heating system is of great benefit to anyone taking a shower on board outside summer; most caravans that have the option of running the space heater on electricity will have this facility. When you turn on the heater's electric function, you can set the fan control on top of the heater itself to dispense blown air – at a temperature controlled by you – to each of the low-level outlets in the caravan. Typically, there will be one in the front lounge, one in the side and/or rear lounge/bedroom, and one in the washroom. You can close off the others so that the sole destination of all this warm air is the washroom. Give it a five-minute start before you go in for your shower and it really will make a difference to what can be a chilly little room first thing in the morning.

Some posher, more recent caravans have domestic-style central heating, with a radiator in the washroom that looks just like the one in the bathroom at home. That really does smack of being spoiled!

When everyone has finished using the shower, give it a quick but thorough wipe-down and make sure it's well ventilated. There's usually a roof vent to facilitate this and there may be a window, depending on layout.

Some showers on lower-spec caravans utilize the hand-basin's mixer tap: you pull it gently from its aperture at the basin and relocate it on the shower holder. I've never had a problem with this set-up; indeed, it comes into its own for quickly rinsing off sandy feet after a day on the beach.

There are a few caravans where the mixer tap detaches in this manner – but with nowhere to slot it into for taking a shower. This has always struck me as being slightly cruel on the part of the caravan's designers.

Key points

Showering tip no 1: When drying yourself off after a shower, whether in the caravan or the on-site facilities, use your flannel for the bulk of that particular task, saving your towel for a brisk final flourish. You'll find that even such a small area of flannelette is remarkably effective; and you'll be able to keep at bay that caravanning bugbear: damp towels.

Showering tip no 2: If water always seems to collect in one corner of the shower tray instead of draining away, you'll find that a minor adjustment to your caravan's levelling will do the trick (refer back to the earlier section in this chapter for more about levelling). If you're really keen, you can take a lead from a particularly fastidious caravanner I met some years ago. He never quite managed to get rid of every last drop of water after a shower, so he fitted a second drain plug in the diagonally opposite corner from the existing one.

Effective use of water

Unless you have the luxury of a pitch that offers a direct water connection to your caravan (these are few and far between), you have a finite supply of water and so it's in your best interests to be as frugal as possible in your use of it.

If you're caravanning with your family, all of whom are making demands on the supply, you may at first be surprised at how quickly it runs out. There is an unwritten caravanning law stating that the taps will run dry when you least expect them to, when your need is greatest and when the weather is at its most foul.

Here's your survival strategy:

▶ Consider taking two fresh-water containers with you. Fill up both when you arrive and connect one to the caravan in the usual way. Then, if you're caught short, at least you can be 'on tap' again very quickly, just by swapping the submersible from the empty container to the full one.

▶ Don't leave the tap running for a second longer than you have to; as soon as that toothbrush is damp, turn it off. When washing your hands, turn it off after you've applied the soap and then back on again to rinse.

▶ If you actually intend to use the shower (many caravanners never do), look for a type with a mixer tap and a single lever, rather than separate hot and cold taps (a set-up that's now pretty much confined to older vehicles). This means you can set the water to the optimum temperature and turn it off while you lather up, leaving the temperature setting exactly where it is. Then, when you're ready to rinse, just nudge the lever to turn it back on again.

▶ If the fresh-water point is not too far away from where you're pitched – on some sites each pitch will have its own tap – it's good to get into the habit of filling up the kettle or the saucepan directly from there rather than using the caravan's supply. This can make a really noticeable difference to how often you have to fill up your fresh-water containers.

▶ In a similar vein, thoroughly clean and rinse a four- or six-pint plastic milk carton and use it to top up the fresh-water container every so often. Yes, it still means regular trips to the water point, but it cuts down on the amount of times you need to lug the big container there and back. It's also a 'holiday duty' you can get the children involved in.

▶ If you're making a quick overnight stop, perhaps with the need to make a speedy exit the next morning, you can save time and effort by investing in a collapsible, plastic fresh-water container with a tap, which you can place for the night on a worktop in the caravan. That should be more than enough to look after your water requirements for the few hours you'll be on site.

▶ Take the fullest possible advantage of the caravan site's facilities, such as washing-up areas and, of course, the shower/ toilet block.

Effective use of gas

In most countries (including the UK), you pay an all-in pitch fee that includes your mains electricity hook-up. In the majority of caravans, this gives you the means to cut down on your gas usage quite dramatically. For example, most caravans' space heaters run on either gas or mains electricity, so if you need to have the heater on, switch it to electric (in winter, leaving it on the lowest setting overnight is enough to keep the chill at bay). The same applies for the water heater. Many caravans now have cooker hobs with three gas rings and one electric hotplate.

Even if your caravan is equipped with a gas-only space heater, bring along a small, low-wattage electric fan heater and use that whenever possible. If your caravan is equipped with a gas-only water heater, use your electric kettle to heat some water if all you want is a modest amount for washing-up or to have a quick freshen-up in the washroom.

You can also use your kettle in this way when you need to bring a pan of water to the boil. Let the kettle do this task before you transfer it to the pan and on to the gas hob. It's quicker as well as more economical. See 'Effective use of mains hook-up' below.

Effective use of your fridge

A fully functioning fridge is more of a necessity than a luxury, especially if you're caravanning in hot weather. Your perishable items will stay unperished for longer and you'll really appreciate those cold beers as you swelter over a hot barbecue in the sultry evenings. Here's how to make the most of this vital piece of equipment:

▶ Caravan fridges are painfully slow to reach optimum operating temperature, but there are ways you can alleviate this. In Chapter 5, we discussed how the grey 12S electrical lead, when connected to the same-coloured socket on the towcar, powers the fridge from the car battery when the car's ignition is switched on. Take the fullest-possible advantage of this fact: if you're making a journey of any length, you should have a nicely chilled cabinet by the time you reach the site.

▶ If you have the caravan at home prior to setting off, you can connect it to your house's mains electricity system, using a cheap adaptor from your nearest caravan accessory shop. Plug in and get the fridge running overnight and/or while you load up the caravan for the journey.

▶ Remember to remove the protective covers (if fitted) from the fridge vents on the exterior wall, or you won't get anything like optimum performance from it. These covers should only be left in place when caravanning in the winter, in order to stop the fridge from over-freezing.

▶ Two tips in one: a couple of days before you leave on holiday, cook a big casserole (or other favourite dish that can be frozen), place it in a suitable container and freeze it. Just before you set off, put it in the caravan fridge and run the fridge from the car battery as you travel. The frozen food will make a big difference to the time it takes for the fridge to run cold and, of course, it's thawing all the time, ready to provide your first night's meal and saving you the chore of having to cook after setting up the caravan.

▶ Some fridges have a token ice-making box rather than a full-width freezer compartment. This is a definite minus, especially in hot weather, when your fridge is having to work overtime to keep things tolerably cool. If you like your white wine chilled, you will need that full-width freezer.

Key point

How trustworthy is a milk carton that has already been opened? 'Not very' is the correct answer. If it should get knocked over in the fridge while you're travelling and start leaking, it will make an awful mess and cause a smell that will linger for months. Always have at least one airtight plastic container to hand, so that you can transfer milk (or juice) into it for secure transit.

Remember this

There's been a welcome trend in recent years towards bigger-capacity caravan fridges. Even so, it can still be a challenge to fit everything in. Many families take some of the pressure off by having a secondary camping-style portable fridge set up in the awning. That's a good solution, but as these fridges are both bulky and heavy, make sure you're not overloading the caravan if you take one with you.

Effective use of mains hook-up

Most caravans are equipped to operate happily without being connected to a mains electricity supply for a few days. Most sites, though, offer a mains hook-up facility, and the overwhelming majority of caravanners take advantage of it to run a range of appliances that are either built in or brought along by them.

You will need to take account of the ampere (or amp) rating of the site's electricity supply – in other words, the quantity of electrical current passing through a cable. If you run so many appliances at once that you exceed the site's rating, you will overload the system and the electricity supply will cut out. You'll then need to ask the site warden to reconnect you – a minor inconvenience at best, but a positive nuisance if it happens late at night and you have to wait until the next day to get an electricity supply again.

It's worth noting that it may not just be you who loses the supply, but anyone else who has connected to the same post as you and, in some instances, the entire site. If this happens, keep a low profile and pretend it wasn't you!

Luckily, some simple arithmetic is all that's required to make sure you avoid this uncomfortable scenario and stay safely connected.

▶ First, find out what the site's electricity supply amp-rating is. Most UK sites are quite generous, varying between 10 and 16 amps – the latter figure is the highest possible in the UK, and is common on club sites. The amperage of overseas sites is usually lower, with 6 amps not uncommon. Some off-the-beaten-track sites on the continent may even offer only a 4-amp hook-up.

▶ Remember this formula: amps = watts ÷ volts. So, if you combine the total wattage (energy output) of the appliances you intend to use at any one time and divide the total by 230 (the UK mains electricity system is rated at 230 volts), you have the amps figure you need to compare with that of the site you're staying on.

▶ Don't forget to take account of those appliances that are usually always on, typically the fridge (which takes up about 100 watts of your allowance) and the on-board battery charger (no more than about 300 watts).

For example, let's assume we're hooked up to the electricity supply of a site that's rated at 10 amps. We want to run the following:

fridge	100 watts
battery charger	300 watts
colour TV	90 watts
table lamp	60 watts
kettle	750 watts
space heater	1,000 watts
Total	*2,300 watts*

So, 2,300 ÷ 230 = 10. In other words, we'll be using up 10 amps, which is our absolute ceiling – and therefore too risky. It may just cause the supply to cut out.

But there's an easy solution. As you can see, the space heater is especially power-hungry on its electric setting, so switch it off (or operate it on gas) while the kettle boils.

The kettle, even the low-wattage model used in this example, is also quite greedy. If we were staying on that 4-amp site in rural France, for example, the combined total of running the fridge and battery charger while boiling the kettle would amount to about 5 amps and therefore trip the supply.

Key point

To save you from doing the same sums over and over again, use the formula given here (i.e. amps = watts ÷ volts) to calculate the amperage of all the electrical appliances you normally use, write these figures down on a piece of card and attach it to the inside of a locker door for easy reference.

Toilet training

Please don't lose any sleep worrying about having to endure primitive sanitary arrangements when you're living in your caravan. The cassette toilet has been around for decades now, and its simple, clinical efficiency makes visits to your caravan's smallest room extremely civilized.

However, there's no escaping the fact that the necessary emptying of the cassette isn't anybody's idea of a great job, even though some sites make it as fuss-free as possible by providing discreet, well-equipped chemical toilet disposal points. Do be warned, though: although every single site must provide some means of chemical disposal, at the most basic establishments this may amount to no more than a covered drain in the corner of a field.

Your caravan accessory shop will stock two types of chemical fluid. The important one is added directly to the reservoir of the cassette, in a quantity that will be specified on the container. This fluid is essential to the hygienic operation of the toilet. The other one, usually coloured pink, is added to the flushing water tank and serves no purpose other than to impart a nice, perfumed smell.

▶ Buy toilet chemicals in bulk – not only are they much cheaper, but it can be hard to find replacements in out-of-the-way places, especially overseas. Don't, whatever you do, run out of toilet chemicals!

▶ Before you set off towing, place sufficient water in the flushing tank, and a little water/chemical mixture in the reservoir – this ensures that the toilet is set up for use en route.

▶ Before you use a cassette toilet, you need to operate a lever that slides open the blade separating reservoir from toilet bowl. This is an operation best performed with the lid down.

▶ Depending on which type your caravan is fitted with, the toilet is flushed either manually by pumping a lever up and down a couple of times, or electrically by pushing a button. Those with restricted movement in their hands, due to arthritis, for example, will find it much easier to use the electric-flush type.

▶ Don't wait until the cassette is brim-full before emptying it at the dedicated facility. An LED (light-emitting diode) or coloured bar on the side of the unit will warn when the reservoir is full, but it really is best to pre-empt this if you can.

▶ Many caravanners set strict house rules when it comes to the use of the on-board toilet, e.g. that the site's own facilities should be used instead whenever possible.

Some makes of wheeled waste-water containers are shaped specifically to accommodate a cassette toilet, which is secured by elastic cord. The idea – a good one – is that you can empty both in one visit to the site's facilities, and you're also spared the considerable effort involved in lugging a nearly full cassette around.

However civilized the operation of emptying a toilet may be, you may understandably decide that being allocated a pitch adjacent to the facility where this takes place is not right for you. Ask to be given an alternative pitch.

Keeping it all tidy

Before you know it, your caravan can start to look cluttered unless you adopt a 'place for everything, everything in its place' policy. There's nothing worse than trying to find the car keys ('but I thought you had them last ...') when you're all packed and ready to go out for the day.

▶ Keys play a big part in a caravan holiday: car keys, caravan keys, security device keys, site barrier key (or pass), maybe even a shower-block key if the site has such a policy. As such, decide where in the caravan these keys should live – and stick to it religiously. Some caravans have a narrow shelf above the entrance door – that's perfect.

▶ Coats and jackets take up a huge amount of room, so either keep them in the awning or shut away in the boot of the car.

▶ When you go out for the day, don't leave valuables in the awning if they can't be secured. Wallets, passports, MP3 players, mobile phones, cameras and games consoles etc. should either be taken with you or locked away out of sight in the caravan.

▶ To help cut down on the amount of foodstuffs that you have to store in the caravan, buy smaller packs and jars, or decant from home into more compact containers. For example, why bring (or buy on-site) a big, bulky box of washing powder when you're probably only going to use a couple of handfuls all the time you're away?

▶ If you're only going away for the weekend, you can take this policy even further by putting a weekend's worth of rice, pasta, cereal and such like into freezer bags and securing them with ties or clips; it'll take up substantially less space and bulk, helping you to travel lighter and have a clutter-free weekend.

▶ One of the benefits of a caravan with a permanent double bed is the veritable chasm of storage space that's available underneath it. On most models, the bed base lifts up easily and supports itself on a gas-assisted strut, making the huge storage area extremely accessible.

Remember this

Some caravans come with a bespoke compact waste bin, often attached to the inside of the entrance door or on the inside of a cupboard door. Lined with a carrier bag, they're a big help in maintaining an orderly caravan interior. If yours doesn't have such a facility, buy a cheap plastic, lidded bin (I use a bin designed to accommodate recyclable food waste at home) and give over a corner of a cupboard to it. Anything's got to be better than the age-old carrier bag hooked over a door handle!

Focus points

The main points to remember from this chapter are:

* Whatever manoeuvre you're undertaking with your caravan, take your time. It's not a race!

* Practise reversing as often as you can. It's not that difficult to master and, once you have done so, it's very satisfying to do. Yet again, take your time.

* When you want to reverse the caravan so that it turns at an angle, turn the steering wheel – initially – in the opposite direction to the way you want the caravan to turn. So, to back the caravan round to the left, turn the steering wheel to the right.

* You'll rarely ever need to be able to reverse the caravan with inch-perfect precision. Let the car do most of the hard work, then guide it by hand into place.

* Don't like the sound of that? Invest in a motorized mover: expensive but effective, especially if your mobility is limited.

* You're bound to encounter an uneven pitch at some time.

* Be prepared for it by keeping some cheap plastic levelling ramps and wheel chocks in the gas locker.

* Before you unhitch the caravan from the car, make sure the caravan's jockey wheel is lowered and clamped tightly.

* If you intend to use a caravan's shower regularly, those models with fully sealed shower compartments offer the best protection against the risk of damp.

* You can cut down on your gas consumption considerably by using the electric function of your caravan's appliances whenever possible.

* Don't risk 'tripping' the site's electricity supply. Calculate which appliances you can use in safety by using the formula: amps = watts ÷ volts.

8

Protecting your investment

In this chapter, you will learn:

▶ *how to protect your caravan from the risk of theft – and where to store it safely*

▶ *what essential DIY tasks you can undertake – and the importance of regular servicing*

▶ *how to prepare your caravan for sale.*

It's a sad fact, but caravans are really easy to steal. Think about it. If you leave it unprotected anywhere – be it on site, on your driveway at home, in storage at a friend's farm, attached to your car in a motorway service area car park – all that a budding villain has to do is to turn up in a vehicle fitted with a towbar and drive off with it.

Because of that, every insurance company will insist that you take at least minimum precautions for your cover to be valid. But, notwithstanding that, it's absolutely crucial that you do what you can to make your caravan as hard to steal as possible. The quality of caravan-specific theft deterrents has improved markedly in recent years, with a large number now coming with Sold Secure approval.

Sold Secure

This is an independent testing body whose team of expert locksmiths set about testing mechanical security devices such as wheel clamps, hitch locks and hitch posts, using the same sort of methods as less well-intentioned types to try to overcome them.

If the devices manage to beat the criteria set down by the organization during this attack-testing, they are granted Sold Secure approval and can promote the fact on their packaging and in their marketing. Buying and fitting such a device – maybe even more than one – is obviously no guarantee that your caravan won't be stolen, but the key word here is 'deterrent'. Sold Secure looks for successful products to have excessive nuisance value, i.e. that the risk of being caught in the act while attempting to overcome an approved device will drive the would-be thief off in search of easier pickings elsewhere.

Maybe there are products out there that are very good quality but which haven't been tested and endorsed by Sold Secure. Fair enough. But my eyes were opened when, having commissioned some expert locksmiths for an article in the caravan magazine I was then editing, I tagged along to watch a wide range of caravan wheel clamps and hitch locks being attack-tested.

We'd asked each supplier to provide two samples of each device. One particular wheel clamp was fitted as per the instructions and the stopwatch began its count. Within seconds it was a pile of useless yellow metal strewn about the car park. The chief tester was certain there must have been something wrong with that sample, so he asked for the other one to be fitted. That became a pile of useless yellow metal even quicker than the first one.

The point being? Play it safe and invest in something that you know has survived a rigorous onslaught.

You'll also see some devices that carry approval from TNO, an organization that does similar work in the Netherlands, caravanning capital of Europe. That, too, is a widely respected body within the industry, so such approval also carries a lot of clout.

Remember this

The lengths that some thieves will go to in order to steal a caravan they've had their evil eye on is remarkable: it surprises even the police. In one case in my local area, they cut a vehicle-sized hole in a hedge, drove across a field to a farm, forced open a locked gate, overcame the caravan's security devices and dragged it back over the field.

The message is clear: don't ever be complacent and assume it won't happen to you.

What security products to fit

I would recommend that you protect your caravan with at least one wheel clamp and a hitch lock at all times. But whatever you decide to fit, make sure it meets or exceeds the requirements set out by your insurer – and if the small print in your policy document falls a long way short of what would be expected by the Plain English Society, call them up and double-check you're covered. The simple truth is that if your caravan is stolen and the insurance assessor finds it wasn't protected in line with the level of your cover, they won't pay out.

WHEEL STANDS: IS YOUR INSURER HAPPY?

Be especially cautious if you fit wheel stands – or 'winter wheels' as they're sometimes called – when laying your caravan up for the off-season. These devices take the place of the conventional wheels, which get whisked off for safe keeping.

The theory is that as well as making sure the tyres don't 'flat-spot' – i.e. become damaged by sitting in the same position for many weeks at a time – the decidedly non-wheel-shaped winter wheels render the caravan immobile, foiling would-be thieves.

Well, this may not be the case, because they can just bring their own wheels with them. A contact in the insurance industry related just such an incident with a caravan belonging to one of his customers. The customer made the claim for theft; it was rejected. The policy stated that the caravan should have a wheel clamp – but the fitment of wheel stands precluded that. So, one null and void insurance policy and one seriously out-of-pocket caravanner. He was doubly unlucky, because locked wheel stands can be an effective deterrent, but his expensive mistake stresses the point that you must check with your insurance company to find out their security-device requirements. Their wishes override yours.

WHEEL CLAMPS

Some wheel clamps give the impression of having been designed by the villains themselves, who are obviously hoping that the amount of hassle involved in manhandling necessarily heavy metal and then trying to decipher jumbled instructions will persuade you not to bother even fitting the thing.

This, too, is a mistake. Ask someone to show you how to fit and – just as importantly – remove the wheel clamp when you buy. Once you've done it a couple of times, you won't have any difficulty.

There are several compact clamps with Sold Secure approval that take less time to attach to a wheel than it takes to read this paragraph. They're ideal for quick coffee stops or toilet breaks en route and, of course, you can fit one of these in addition to your 'main' wheel clamp when you arrive on site.

If your caravan, like the majority of UK-built models, has a chassis manufactured by Al-Ko and alloy wheels, you may be able to take advantage of a compact, easily fitted wheel lock that has also been approved by Sold Secure. This device is highly regarded and easy to use – a nice double-whammy for a security fitment. It's fitted as standard on many models.

The other thing to remember about wheel clamps (indeed, any security device you fit) is to take the spare key with you, but be sure to keep it separate from the master key. One idea is to keep spare caravan and lock keys together in an envelope and hide this somewhere in the car.

HITCH LOCKS
A hitch lock makes a lot of sense. As the name suggests, this is secured in place over the hitch head, preventing the caravan from being attached to a getaway car. Because these are much easier to fit and less cumbersome to carry than wheel clamps, you should look to buy a good-quality hitch lock that can also be fitted when the caravan is still hitched up to the car – ideal for whipping on when you stop off at a service area or pop into the supermarket.

Walk around any caravan site or storage compound and you'll see that many of the wheel clamps and hitch locks in use have covers over them. This isn't just to keep them clean; it makes thieves' lives a whole lot easier if they can identify the security devices they need to overcome. Chances are they've already 'dealt with' a large number of the products on the market, and they'll know which tools of the trade to bring along when they come back to do the dirty deed. If the wheel clamp and/or hitch lock are well-covered, thieves can't identify what deterrents lurk beneath as they make their surreptitious reconnaissance.

Again, it's no guarantee – but it adds another barrier to a thief's modus operandi, which is no bad thing.

Remember this
If you think about it, a caravan is arguably at its most vulnerable in a busy motorway service area car park. With people and vehicles coming and going continually, there's a good chance that brazen thieves can have a caravan unhitched and attached to their own vehicle within a couple of minutes, attracting no attention along the way. If you don't have a hitch lock that you can whip on, leave someone with the caravan at all times. Otherwise, it's at serious risk of going walkies ...

SECURITY POSTS

We'll be looking at the subject of where to store your caravan in more detail later in this chapter, but if you're intending to keep it at home – whether in the garden or on the driveway – a security post is a very worthwhile addition to your armoury. Some even have a towball on top, so that you can secure the caravan to it with a hitch lock.

You can choose posts that simply hinge at the base and lie flat on the ground to allow access over them; others are retractable, being lifted into place from their underground homes when required and being invisible the rest of the time. Again, I recommend the use of any that come with the magic Sold Secure sticker.

Are you on the register?

Almost every new caravan sold in the UK since 1992 is registered with the Caravan Registration and Identification Scheme (CRiS). This means each caravan has a unique 17-digit number that's stamped onto its A-frame (remember, that's the part of the chassis that extrudes from the front of the caravan, containing the hitch-head, handbrake and jockey wheel) and etched onto at least three of the windows. The concept is sound: a thief will have to replace windows and somehow alter the stamped number on the chassis to erase all traces of the caravan's true identity.

Since 1998, the deterrent value of CRiS has been increased by the addition of one or more electronic tags that are concealed within the body of the caravan. These tags, which can be revealed only by special scanners that CRiS makes available to police forces and no one else, also contain that 17-digit number. Any pre-1998 CRiS-registered caravan that hasn't been tagged can have them fitted retrospectively.

Should a caravan be stolen, its details will be stored on the CRiS computer, so there's some protection there for anyone buying a second-hand caravan; for a small fee, a phone call to CRiS (or an online search at www.cris.co.uk) will ascertain whether or not the vehicle is everything the seller says it is.

Marking/identifying your caravan

There are steps you can take in addition to all this to personalize your caravan; marking the roof with a sequence of letters or numbers is worthwhile. If your caravan is stolen and you're able to report it quickly, chances are it'll still be en route to its intended destination – and in the age of the police helicopter, there's a good chance it'll be spotted.

Just a word of caution, though. A few years ago, everybody thought what a good idea it would be to mark the roof of their caravan with their home postcode. But someone, somewhere must have asked the question: 'Doesn't that kind of advertise the fact to a villain who happens to see it – from an overhead bridge or upstairs window or something – that the address bearing that postcode is obviously empty, seeing as how the occupants are away on holiday?'

The answer probably sounded a bit like this: 'You're quite right … don't know why we didn't think of that in the first place. From now on, we'll suggest that any stick-on letters or numbers should be a sequence known only to the owner – part of the caravan's CRiS number or somebody's date of birth, perhaps.'

That advice holds good. Similarly, you can mark various hidden corners of the interior – inside lockers and under beds – with the same sequence. Take lots of photographs of the caravan (always a good idea for any expensive possession), making sure you capture anything that would stand out in any way, even if it happens to be a small chip in the glass door of the oven or that tiny red wine stain on the carpet that looks a bit like a map of France.

Alarm systems

Some posher caravans are fitted with alarms at the factory, while others will have been treated to one by security-conscious owners. You mustn't be tempted to rely on an alarm as your sole theft-prevention measure, though – even if your insurance company would let you get away with doing so.

An alarm (a few of which are Sold Secure-approved) is a valuable ally in your armoury of defences and has an obvious role to play in helping prevent someone breaking into your caravan – which no number of wheel clamps, hitch locks or hidden numbers can do anything about. Just make sure it's fitted properly and that it's not so sensitive that a passing squirrel can set it off from a distance of five metres. If it keeps sounding for no reason, your neighbours will curse and ignore it in equal measure, defeating the whole object somewhat.

Where should you keep your caravan?

This is a big question, which you should address in full before taking the plunge and buying your caravan. Demand for caravan storage outstrips the spaces available in many areas; waiting lists are not uncommon.

So, do your detective bit first. Speak to caravanning neighbours, make a few phone calls ... and read on.

Arguably, the ultimate caravan storage situation would be at home, through some big, high gates at the side of the house and round the back, under cover in a locked outbuilding. Not only does that incur no storage site fees (and they can mount up), but the caravan is out of sight.

This latter attribute is an important one. We've already hinted at one of the main concerns with keeping a caravan at home: if it's in view for 49 weeks of the year and then very obviously not there, that's as good an indication of an empty property as having a week's worth of uncancelled milk bottles accumulating on your front doorstep. It's less of an issue if you have good neighbours who can keep an eye on the place.

TALKING OF NEIGHBOURS ...

... you should consider them before deciding to keep your new arrival at home, too. With the best will in the world, a caravan is not the most subtle thing to have on your drive, towering over your next door neighbour's parked hatchback; or in your back garden, giving the folks at No 43 a fantastic view of it from their once-well-lit new conservatory. It may be that a polite 'we're thinking of getting a caravan' conversation will smooth the path.

Other factors to consider are:

▶ Some housing developments specifically exclude caravans from being kept on any of the properties – check with your local council that no such restrictions apply where you live.

▶ Please remember: it's illegal to park a caravan at the roadside after dark without making sure it's properly lit. You must not leave an unhitched caravan on a public road at any time.

What if you'd like to keep it at home but the street's a bit on the narrow side and, anyway, your drive is on an uphill slope? Such a situation is tailor-made for our good friend, the motorized mover. All you need to do is unhitch in the street and let the battery-powered mover do the rest. With some models, you can stand a few yards away and do the whole thing by remote control: others are effectively battery-powered jockey wheels that you control and steer.

Remember this

A motorized mover is a desirable accessory, without a doubt. But if you aim to buy a twin-axle caravan, it becomes something of a necessity: these beasts take a lot of shifting, even when there are two of you putting your all into it. It almost goes without saying that there are loads of videos demonstrating caravan movers on YouTube.

DEDICATED STORAGE SITES

If keeping your caravan at home is out of the question for some reason, there are a number of other options. Do an online search for 'Caravan storage' and you'll find a list of sites that do just that. These vary widely in quality, from well-meaning individuals with a bit of spare land and a gate with a big padlock, to Alcatraz-like establishments with 24-hour security staff, alarmed gates and CCTV. You may find your caravan on a grassy field that's impossible to get out of without the assistance of four-wheel drive, or it may be indoors in a huge, locked, lit warehouse.

If round-the-clock access is important, make sure such a facility is available. A friend of mine was left in the lurch when a catastrophically delayed ferry from Spain meant he wouldn't be able to return his caravan to the storage site until the early hours. 'Well, you can't bring it round at that time – sorry' was the less-than sympathetic response. A couple of phone calls later, he'd sorted something out with a local campsite, but it made for a pretty stressful end to a holiday. Oh, and he now keeps his caravan somewhere else.

▶ CaSSOA

It's worth drawing your attention to the Caravan Storage Site Owners' Association (CaSSOA). This body has more than 500 member sites throughout Britain that must meet minimum standards of security before being allowed to join. Sites are gold, silver or bronze standard, with those that come in at bronze level being encouraged to upgrade as soon as they can. Some insurers will knock 25 per cent off your premium if you keep your caravan on a CaSSOA site, which will at least offset some of the storage fees.

There's such a demand for storage facilities that many touring caravan sites have set aside areas for this – it's a good business proposition for them, guaranteeing an income all year round, even in the quieter off-season. Make a few calls to some local sites and go and check the lie of the land – literally – for yourself.

Many farmers have also cottoned on to this as a way of putting otherwise redundant land to good use, but standards do vary widely. Some will have embraced security concerns totally to offer high-quality sanctuary, but do be fully aware of what you're doing if you opt for a 'just park it over there behind the muck spreader and it's cash only, thanks' kind of facility.

My uncle keeps his caravan in a storage compound attached to a caravan accessory shop/workshop. If something plays up while he's away in the caravan, he mentions the fact when he returns it to the compound and the problem will be fixed before he next uses it. Clearly, this is a business proposition that suits both parties very well.

Once again – please make sure your insurer gives you the green light before you commit to anything.

Key point

The specialist caravanning magazines – including the two big club magazines – have many pages of caravan insurance adverts in every issue. There's no substitute for doing some online comparisons or phoning around to try to find the best deal, although you may be able to cut out some of the legwork by getting a friend or contact's recommendation. When you do take out cover, take time to read the small print in your policy – people can, and do, get caught out by not complying with policy conditions.

Keeping it all working

An annual service will keep your caravan safe and legal, but there are a few basic tasks you can undertake yourself to maintain your caravan in first-class condition.

This is a facet of caravan ownership I've always enjoyed: spending a quiet couple of hours with the caravan on a Saturday afternoon, coffee to hand and the football commentary on the radio, is a decidedly therapeutic activity. You'll very quickly find that there's a tremendous pride of ownership involved in having a caravan. Here are the kind of things you should be looking out for in between your mugs of coffee.

TYRES

These are, without question, the most overlooked components on a caravan – which is incredible, given the critical role they play. We ask an awful lot of these two (or four) small hoops of rubber and they really don't need much in return.

Tyre pressures are important for safe, efficient performance; under- or over-inflation not only increases wear, it increases the risk of instability. Use a reliable pressure gauge to ensure that your caravan's tyres meet the manufacturer's recommendation – you'll find this in the owner's handbook. Some manufacturers helpfully stamp the correct pressure on the wheel arch, which is a commendable, common-sense touch. Making it so prominent also acts as a continual reminder to get the gauge out and do the decent thing.

If a tyre is over-inflated, you can deflate it by pushing the top of the dust cap on to the valve. Do it a little at a time, until the gauge gives you the correct reading. If you need to put some air in, a foot pump is all you need; there's not a lot of effort involved in topping up a small caravan tyre. Go for a twin-barrel pump, which emits a greater volume of air with every stroke than a cheaper, single-barrel one.

While you're at it, don't forget the spare tyre which – out of sight, out of mind and all that – tends to be even more neglected than the others.

If your caravan is staying put for a while, take the opportunity while the wheel clamp's off to move it forward or backward by a couple of inches. This will eliminate the risk of a flat spot forming on the tyre due to standing in one position for a long time.

Remember this

Have you changed a wheel on your caravan yet? Do you know the best place to position the jack for safe operation? Do you know for sure that the caravan's wheel nuts will loosen when you apply some muscle with the wheel brace? Is the caravan's spare wheel easy to release from its cradle? If the answer to any of these questions is 'no', put that right. I wouldn't wish to be trying out a wheel-change operation on my caravan for the first time on the hard shoulder. In the rain. At dusk. Practise it when there's no pressure on.

Caravan tyres usually look like they have years of service left in them – after all, they don't do a huge annual mileage compared to most car wheels. But there's a hidden risk. All tyres deteriorate with age, regardless of use, and a caravan's tyres are particularly vulnerable because of the amount of time they sit there doing nothing except get exposed to extreme weather, be it baking sun or harsh frost. Over time, this weakens the sidewalls – you may even, on close inspection, see cracks appearing.

So, make sure you inspect the tyres regularly and thoroughly for any signs of deterioration on the sidewalls; and use a penknife or small screwdriver to flick out any stones or other objects that have become embedded in the tread.

Even if the tyres look fine, replace them as a matter of course every seven years – in line with guidelines set by the British Tyre Manufacturers' Association. As we discussed in Chapter 1, if you buy a second-hand caravan that's four or more years old, make it a priority to fit new tyres to it unless the seller can show you the receipt that proves the existing ones are still youthful enough to be serviceable. And always choose whatever fitment your caravan manufacturer recommends. There's nothing to be gained by 'upgrading' to something with a lower profile.

KEEP IT WELL-OILED

A lot of moving parts on a caravan will cease to do their job if you don't apply regular lubrication. As well as making life much easier for you, prospective purchasers of your caravan in years to come will feel very well-disposed towards it as they glide the corner steadies up and down again in smooth silence. By the time they experience the seamless, silken operation of the jockey wheel handle, they'll be reaching for their wallets.

Oil and grease can be messy things to handle, so a big box of latex gloves from the local DIY emporium is a wise investment. Never used them? Trust me – you'll wonder how you ever managed without them. Remounting a drive-chain on a bicycle, slapping a coat of varnish on an old chair, removing dust caps from grime-laden wheels... they make so many everyday jobs that much more civilized. The best ones have a delicate dusting of talcum powder to ease their removal – a worthwhile attribute to look out for.

So, with latex gloves duly donned, you can dip your fingers into the pot of grease you also bought from the DIY emporium and smear a modest amount along the length of the rotating screw of each of the corner steadies. And before you take the gloves off, do the same to the moving parts of the underslung spare-wheel carrier if your caravan has such a thing.

Lubricate the jockey wheel winder and the clamp with a few dabs of light oil, and make sure both can move easily while you're doing so. If your caravan is stored on level ground, with the corner steadies lowered, don't leave the handbrake on for weeks at a time as this applies unnecessary tension to the cable.

Squeaky doors inside the caravan can be cured in a trice by treating the errant hinges to a gentle smear of olive oil. You can also do the same to free up reluctant push-button door catches.

AND KEEP IT CLEAN, TOO

For many caravanners, this is a real labour of love – but there's no need to go overboard. A good going-over with a proprietary caravan cleaner three or four times a year, including at the start of the season, will keep it looking smart. If you want to go the extra mile, lavishing the bodywork with a wax cleaner will give it a showroom gloss.

Some storage sites offer the facility of a platform that allows easy access to the roof, which can otherwise be awkward to reach.

Yes, a stepladder and an extended washing brush from the caravan accessory shop will probably suffice, but be careful not to get carried away and lean against the roof with all your weight – not unless said roof is made of thick-gauge aluminium that gives you the option of standing on it (should you really want to).

Most caravan windows are acrylic double-glazed items that are easy enough to clean. For best results, I'd avoid using a sponge on dirty windows, and dry them off with a chamois leather or similar. If you get irritating deposits of tar on your windows, don't scrape away at them with your fingernails – pick up some tar remover from a DIY store.

Inside, you can keep everything spick and span by using exactly the same products you would when doing the housework at home. The walls and ceiling will require no more than an occasional wipe-over with a damp cloth.

If your caravan has removable carpets, take full advantage of this: leave them at home if you're going on a beach holiday with the family or to a grassy rally site after a period of heavy rain. Five minutes – actually, make that three minutes – with a damp cloth and a dustpan and brush will restore even the sandiest, muckiest floor to its pristine best.

Being conscientious bordering on neurotic when packing away kitchen store-cupboard items before towing will reward you by not making it necessary to undertake cleaning assignments of a more dramatic nature. Don't fall prey to what happened to this caravanner.

Case study

'We were on a tour of Ireland with a group of friends. Some of Ireland's smaller roads can be rather bumpy and, in the course of negotiating them, this bag of sugar head-butted its way out of the locker and on to the work surface below, bursting free.

'We didn't find it until we opened the caravan door hours later – and I still can't believe what a mess it had made. It was everywhere.

'It took hours to clean, even with the help of a vacuum cleaner supplied by the site owner, and each new journey over the next few days flushed more sugar out. We kept on finding it for weeks afterwards.'

It could have been worse. A heavyweight jar of jam or marmalade, as well as having the potential to cause an equally spectacular mess, would probably have left an unsightly – and permanent – dent in the worktop. And it would be there, staring up at you every time you used the caravan.

The moral is clear: don't store anything heavy, fragile or potentially messy in an overhead locker when you're on the move. If you can move it around, it will move around when you're under way.

APPROVED CARAVAN WORKSHOPS

This network was set up some years ago by the National Caravan Council, the UK's industry body, to address the issue of poor-quality caravan service standards. The requirement that workshops have to meet important criteria – both in terms of customer guarantees and work carried out on the caravan during an approved service – means the scheme has gained the backing of prominent organizations such as the Caravan Club and the Camping and Caravanning Club, although each provider is assessed and inspected by an independent firm.

At the time of writing, the scheme's operators have approved more than 300 workshops around the UK as approved workshops. To check the location of the one nearest to your home, log on to www.approvedworkshops.co.uk or call 01252 796055. You may not even have to travel anywhere: the scheme covers mobile as well as fixed workshops.

Oh, and don't nonchalantly call up a service centre looking to book your caravan in the week before you're due to go on your first long holiday. Waiting lists at some of the busier establishments are notoriously long, stretching into many weeks; it's better to aim for a date in winter or early spring.

If you know of an outlet locally that's not a member of the scheme but which comes highly recommended by caravanners who have used it and continue to do so, that's probably just as valid.

Some owners are more than happy to travel a long distance to have their caravan serviced by someone they know will do a good job, who can carry out the work at far shorter notice than anywhere within reasonable striking distance of their home and who can return the caravan to the happy customer after only a few hours' wait. You may consider one long day to be less of an inconvenience than having to drop the caravan off one day and come back for it the next.

Preparing for winter storage

You're missing a trick if you send your caravan into hibernation for the winter. An increasing number of sites stay open all year round, and the countryside can be just as enticing on a bracingly clear winter's day as it can be in midsummer. Chances are, you'll have it all to yourself as well.

Not convinced? Well, if you are going to lay up the caravan over the winter months, you'll need to take a few simple precautions to ward off unpleasant surprises when you take it out of mothballs come the onset of spring.

The main thing you have to keep at bay is condensation – the principal cause of dampness taking hold in a caravan. If you can, remove all the pieces of soft furnishing and store them in the spare room at home. If that's not an option, stand them up lengthways in the caravan to let the air get to them. For the same reason, open all cupboard and locker doors.

If you want a definition of a tenner well-spent, here's my nomination: a little plastic moisture trap with some spare crystals to add when the time comes to reuse it. The first time I used one of these (any caravan accessory shop will stock them), I was absolutely amazed how much moisture it had drawn in over the course of a couple of weeks or so – a brilliantly cost-effective means of keeping damp at bay. It's a good idea to slip on your (now-invaluable) latex gloves while handling these crystals, because they may cause mild irritation if they come into contact with your skin.

Give the fridge a good clean-out (take all the removable shelves and trays home to wash them) and leave the door ajar by flicking on the travel lock. Forget to do this and you'll have a major cleaning job on your hands in a mildewy kind of way.

If you walk around some second-hand caravans on a dealer's forecourt, you can instantly spot the ones that have been stored over winter with the blinds up or the curtains open; those areas of furniture exposed to the sun (such as it is in winter, admittedly) will have a bleached, faded look that really drags down the overall appearance.

If you're leaving the battery in situ, treat it to at least one full charge during the lay-up (unless you have a solar panel fitted). If you can't do this at its place of storage, take it out and do it at home.

Make sure you drain every drop of water from the caravan to eliminate the risk of frost damage. Open the drain plug adjacent to the water heater to allow any contents to run out, and open both the hot and cold taps. It helps if you can do this when the water heater is still warm.

If you're undertaking this particular operation when there's still a fair amount of water in the system, you should first open all the hot and cold taps on board to let the bulk of the water drain into your waste-water container.

Make sure the fresh-water supply for the loo has all been flushed away and the holding tank emptied. When you slot the tank back into place, go back into the washroom and slide the blade open.

As a final water-purging exercise, lower and raise the caravan by winding the jockey wheel handle. You may be surprised to find how much water this liberates from the pipework; water that would otherwise inevitably freeze up.

Give the interior a thorough clean – including the kitchen appliances. If you don't have access to hot water for wiping surfaces and rinsing cloths, bring a flask of hot water with you from home.

If you have a say in the matter, be choosy where you leave your caravan. If it's on grass, for example, don't let it grow to the extent that it can block the floor-level vents, because this is another potential route for damp to get inside. Also, be wary of its proximity to trees; if a fierce storm brings down some hefty branches, it's bound to be your caravan they end up denting, not the one next to it. And regular deliveries of soggy leaves, tree sap and bird droppings on to your caravan's roof will do nothing to enhance its appearance.

Don't allow the caravan to sit on its tyres in one place for long periods of time. Three or four times over the winter, move it so that the wheels revolve by at least half a turn. While you're there, open all the doors, windows and sunroofs to treat the caravan to a healthy session of ventilation. Before you go home, make sure you've left the handbrake off – lower the corner steadies instead.

Remember this

One last crack at persuading you to have a couple of winter weekends away in your caravan ... Even if you don't go very far, it's a great opportunity to give all the moving parts (wheels, brakes, steady winders, interior doors and so on) a good work-out, not to mention keeping all the various appliances in good health. Oh, and you'll enjoy it, too.

Ready to sell?

If you've been suitably fastidious with your beloved caravan, you can expect to find a buyer for it easily when the time comes to sell. Brand-new caravans, desirable though they are, are expensive and, because that puts them beyond the reach of many, there's a constant, ready market for second-hand tourers in good condition.

In particular, the second-hand market is always buoyant among younger buyers with families, so if you're attempting to shift a four-, five- or six-berth caravan, chances are it'll be on its way to a new home even quicker than a two-berth model.

Of course, you have the same choices as a seller that you had as a buyer: do it privately or use the services of a dealer. Some dealers will agree to sell it on your behalf, i.e. the caravan remains your property until it's sold, at which point the dealer receives a commission.

SELLING TO A DEALER

If you're looking to do a trade-in – using your caravan to part-finance the purchase of another – selling to a dealer is undoubtedly the most hassle-free, straightforward option. If you want simply to sell the caravan to the dealer without buying another from him, that's fine as well – but be prepared to accept a lower price.

The most important thing to remember when trading in a caravan for a replacement is not to get too fixated on the trade-in price. Instead, focus on the 'price to change' – how much money you will have to spend to complete the transaction.

For example, a dealer may offer you £1,000 for your caravan as part-payment towards a new one that costs £10,000 and which he insists he can't give you a discount on. That means you're going to have to pay £9,000.

Maybe he'll offer you £500 for your caravan, which seems disappointing at first – but then he agrees to sell you the £10,000 new model for £9,500. Price to pay? Still £9,000. How he chooses to conduct the transaction really doesn't matter a jot. What matters to you is the amount that your bank account will be lighter by.

Whether you're selling privately or to a dealer, don't expect to recoup money on the strength of accessories you've added to the caravan during the time you've owned it. The two possible exceptions to this are a motorized mover and an awning.

If the price to change still seems a bit on the high side but you're genuinely keen to do a deal, a good salesperson will pick up on this. He or she won't be keen to lose a nearly completed sale, so it's always worthwhile seeing what you can negotiate. Even if there's no more room for manoeuvre on the price to change, maybe you can have an extra year's warranty thrown in. How about including your first year's service as part of the price? What about that nice gas barbecue you saw in the accessory shop?

SELLING PRIVATELY ... ON EBAY

You have a few options if you choose to sell the caravan yourself. Locally or nationally? Car-led mart publications or caravanning specialist press? And what about the internet?

What about it indeed. Let's start there first. Perhaps you'd rather work an extra shift down the pit for no money than sell anything on eBay, but it can be an effective showroom for your caravan and is, at the very least, worth having a look at – even if it's just to see how other sellers are faring with their vehicles. If you don't own a computer, feel free to skip the next few paragraphs ...

I've just had a quick look on eBay and there are a staggering 1,457 used caravans for sale there – most are classified-style ads with no bidding involved, but nearly 300 are looking for a highest bidder. A 2003 Avondale Rialto two-berther has just been sold for £2,500, having attracted a very healthy 29 bids.

A similar number of bids were attracted by a 1992 five-berth Lunar Premier 515 SE, which included a full awning described as being in 'as new' condition, and a host of other extras such as a 24-inch LCD TV with Freesat receiver and dish. Photos suggested it was as dry and clean as the seller suggested. It went for £1,577 – which almost makes me wish I'd chanced upon it a bit earlier. This proves just what a bargain you can find if you're in the right place at the right time – and both these examples show what healthy interest you can drum up on eBay if you're selling a decent-quality product.

Not every caravan attracts such interest, of course, but if you advertised yours for sale in the local paper and received nearly 30 calls enquiring after it, you'd probably be really pleased.

If you've never tried selling on eBay before, why not give it a go by putting up something of modest value – a DVD you know you'll never watch again, maybe – just to see how it all works? It's fun to monitor the progress of your item, especially as the seconds tick down to the end of the time you've allocated for it.

My quick scan showed that some buyers were being a little optimistic with their asking prices. Do your research and see amounts what other caravans of the same type and age are being advertised for, whether on eBay or in print. How you structure the auction is up to you. You can put the caravan up for three days if you're confident of a quick sale, or you can go for something like seven or ten days if you want to give as many potential buyers as possible an opportunity to see it.

Again, if you're feeling confident, you can offer it for sale with no reserve, i.e. the highest bid gets the caravan, even though that could turn out to be £4.99. In reality, it can be a good sales ploy because it encourages people to slap in bids, which in turn attracts other surfers when they see that there's a bit of interest being shown in a particular caravan.

It's rare for a no-reserve item to sell for much less than its real-world value. Sometimes, people get a bit carried away and bid over the odds, much to the delight of the seller as he or she monitors every twist and turn.

If you want to play it more cautiously, you can put a reserve price on the caravan to make absolutely certain that you're not on the wrong end of a freakishly low bid. The trick here, though, is not to make the reserve too high. If you're selling a caravan for which you want £3,000 and you set the reserve at £2,800, bidders can lose interest. Advertising a caravan with a 'low reserve price' encourages people in.

In the above example, a reserve of £2,000 could be considered low and, unless you were really unlucky, you could expect to get more for it than that. Bidders don't get to know what reserve price you've set – until someone has bid an amount that meets or exceeds it.

From a security point of view, there's little difference between eBay and any other kind of private sale. It's only right that potential buyers will want to come and see the caravan, so you may care to make a rendezvous at a busy motorway service area car park or somewhere else well populated if you don't want callers to know where it's being stored.

You can attach a 'buy it now' price to the caravan, potentially attracting a keen buyer who doesn't want to risk losing out. But do your homework – look at what similar caravans have sold for by ticking the 'show completed listings' box.

SELLING PRIVATELY ... BY MORE TRADITIONAL MEANS
Local newspapers continue to be a popular means of advertising vehicles. They're a traditional, trusted source and buyers know they won't have to travel too far to view the items. Unlike the wide-open spaces of eBay, though, where you can write a short story to describe the item and illustrate it with the contents of an entire memory card, you'll have to be choosy for a newspaper ad, making every one of your allotted 30 or so words count – and hope that the minuscule photograph that's printed does the caravan justice.

But it's being local that's the trump card. If all you say in the ad is that the caravan is in VGC (very good condition), that's more than enough for potential buyers to make the ten-minute drive to find out its actual condition for themselves.

If you think your caravan is that bit special – unusually pristine for an older model, say – or if you want to reach potential buyers who are as enthusiastic about caravans as you are, you can try advertising in the specialist press. The argument for taking this route is that the people looking at your ad are possibly more likely to appreciate your caravan for what it is rather than dismiss it purely because it looks too expensive.

The Camping and Caravanning Club and (especially) the Caravan Club publications have an enormous reach.

GETTING THE MONEY

There's little risk when it comes to being paid. You can specify payment by a banker's draft or building society cheque and say that you won't release the caravan until those funds have cleared. This is an important proviso if you agree to accept payment by this means – elaborate forgeries are not unknown.

An even more secure – and more immediate – means of payment when buying or selling on eBay is to use the PayPal system. In simple terms, this transfers the agreed amount electronically from the buyer's PayPal account into the seller's – and you can see by checking your account details online that the money has been credited to your nominated account.

Still prefer to see lots of £20 notes being counted into your palm? That's fine. You can opt for cash on delivery, too.

Cost-wise, eBay compares reasonably well. The seller of that £2,500 Lunar will have paid about £35. You can include lots of digital photos in your entry, paying a little extra only if you want them to be supersized.

If your caravan doesn't sell – whether due to receiving no bids or the reserve price not being met – you pay just a listings fee which, at the time of writing, is £10 for vehicles.

One note of warning regarding selling a vehicle on eBay with no reserve: don't do it in the build-up to Christmas. At that time of year, people's disposable income tends to be ring-fenced for the always-expensive extended festive season, cutting down on the number of bidders – and you may inadvertently be giving someone an early Christmas present.

That worked spectacularly well for me a couple of years ago when I put in a hugely optimistic bid for a Land Rover and could barely believe it when I won the auction, landing the lovely old thing for what was effectively half its value. But that's another story.

Focus points

The main points to remember from this chapter are:

✳ Look out for security products that bear the Sold Secure logo. They'll have undergone rigorous 'attack-testing' to gain it.

✳ Read your caravan insurance policy's small print all the way through and make sure you comply with its requirements to the letter. Otherwise you risk a no-pay-out situation in the event of a claim.

✳ Don't leave your caravan unprotected in motorway service areas – fit a hitch lock that can be used when the caravan's still attached to the car.

✳ If you're security-marking your caravan's roof, don't use your postcode.

✳ Can't or don't wish to store your caravan at home? Research your storage site options before you buy it.

✳ Never neglect your caravan's tyres. Check their pressure regularly and inspect for signs of damage when you do so. Don't forget the spare.

✳ Keep your caravan looking good: bespoke caravan cleaners work very well.

✳ Keep your caravan well-maintained. There's a nationwide network of Approved Caravan Workshops that must comply with set criteria when servicing your vehicle.

✳ Laying your caravan up for the winter? Make sure it's well-prepared for it – drain fluids, remove upholstery, air it occasionally, don't let the grass grow under its feet (literally ...).

✳ eBay can be a good way of buying or selling a caravan. For buying, there's usually a good choice; for selling, the potential reach is enormous.

9

What it's all about – the joys of touring in the UK

In this chapter, you will learn:

▶ *what to consider when planning your next trip – where the adventure starts*
▶ *some ideas for touring holidays in the UK*
▶ *what to bear in mind if you intend to tour all year long.*

'Where shall we go next?'

That's a question you'll soon be very familiar with after you've bought your caravan. Of course, ownership of a caravan isn't the only means of holidaying in different places every time you go away, but it does bring with it an independence that's inhibited only by your sense of adventure and available pitches on the site(s) you want to stay at.

You'll find yourself watching a TV drama filmed in a particularly scenic part of the country and wondering if there's a good site somewhere in the area (there will be). You'll read a favourable review of an idyllic region of France in one of the Sunday newspaper travel supplements and wonder if it's easy to take a caravan there (it will be).

That's how it is with caravanning. You may only just have returned from holiday, but you'll usually be thinking about the next trip and, working on the old adage that it's always nice to have something to look forward to, you'll be doing so with a smile on your face.

There's no need to plan absolutely every last detail, down to where you'll be going on any given day during your trip away, but there's an undeniable pleasure to be taken from sitting at home on a stormy winter's night, leafing through a pile of sites guides, maps, printouts from websites and brochures from tourist offices, weighing up the pros and cons of Provence or Tuscany ... or Skegness or Cleethorpes.

Key point

Buy a cheap, plastic folder from the stationery shop and start filling it with touring ideas. For example, a review of a particularly wonderful caravan site in the Trossachs; maybe a magazine article about the delights of the Tarka Trail in Devon; some tourist leaflets you picked up from the information desk of the last site you stayed at; or even a scrap of paper with a hastily scribbled reminder to find out more about city breaks in Brussels after being inspired to do so by a radio or TV programme.

DRAW UP YOUR SHORTLIST OF SITES

You'll no doubt have your own list of all the places you want to visit in the caravan. The specialist magazines can be helpful in recommending good-quality sites to stay at, thus minimizing the chances of your holiday being spoiled somewhat by a disappointing one.

When starting to plan your next trip, compiling a shortlist of two or three good (or potentially good) sites in the area you're considering should be the first thing you do. At the end of a tiring day's sightseeing or fell walking, it's a great feeling to be able to look forward to driving back to a site that's clean, pleasant and welcoming – you'll get so much more out of your visit if you can achieve this.

You can compare it to a restaurant where the food is better than anything you've ever tasted, but which is let down by surly service and a cramped, uncomfortable dining room. You'll have paid a lot of money for your gourmet meal, but you'll feel short-changed.

Many sites have their own websites, and while you're not going to get an unbiased, warts-and-all review from that particular source, you'll at least be able to peruse the range of facilities on offer and maybe even check availability. There's no shortage of caravanning-related forums on the internet, where fellow surfers may be able to recommend – or, just as importantly, steer you away from – certain caravan sites.

If you key the name of any given caravan site into an internet search engine – Google being the predominant example – you will often be able to find independent reviews from people who have stayed there. It would be foolish to dismiss an otherwise promising site on the basis of one poor review from a source of unknown reputation; but if there are two or more bad reviews, all offering up the same criticisms, there's arguably cause to pay heed to them.

Arm yourself with a good-quality site guide as a final arbiter of quality, but make sure you choose one in which the listed sites are visited by inspectors and the subsequent reviews updated regularly.

Part of the membership package of both of the UK's major clubs – the Caravan Club, and the Camping and Caravanning Club – is a substantial discount on pitch fees on their own sites. For this reason alone, taking out membership of one or other of these clubs (and in some cases, both) is a sensible step if you plan to tour in the UK with any regularity, because each has a huge network of sites that pretty much covers the entire country. At the time of going to press, the Caravan Club has more than 200 sites, the Camping and Caravanning Club about half that.

Many caravanners are happy to spend entire holidays staying on club sites because they offer more or less uniformly high standards of presentation and provision of facilities. The fact that they are usually managed by employees who are themselves enthusiastic caravanners means a lot to many people, too.

For exactly the same reasons, club sites make exceptionally good stopovers – you know everything will be to club standard and that you'll get a quiet night's rest before continuing your journey the next morning.

The sites guides of both clubs include ideas for days out while staying at each site, and their monthly magazines also include touring features to provide a dash of inspiration.

Remember this

While most Caravan Club and Camping and Caravanning Club sites welcome non-members, some are open to members only, maybe because of their small size or the fact that the facilities are a bit more basic than others. Some of those sites are in very pretty locations, though, so access to them is a real member benefit.

PLAN A GREAT ROUTE

The definition of 'great' depends on your needs. Do you simply want to get to where you're going as quickly and efficiently as possible? Or do you fancy making the journey part of the holiday itself, choosing a more scenic route and perhaps building in an overnight stop or two?

Whichever option you choose, remember to take account of the fact that there's a caravan coming along for the ride too – so, to a greater or lesser extent, your average speed will be lower.

Even if your outfit is beautifully matched and can keep up easily with other traffic, you need to observe the slightly lower speed limits for vehicles with trailers. Not only that, but your overtaking options are obviously very limited on single-carriageway roads.

My best advice if you find yourself stuck behind a frustratingly dawdling driver – no doubt with a lengthening queue of traffic behind you – is to pull over into a lay-by as soon as you can and let the convoy get on its way. It's a good opportunity to stretch your legs and to check that your electrical leads are still connected okay and that the jockey wheel clamp is good and tight. Rejoin the road when there's a decent gap in the traffic, enjoying the fact that it's much more relaxing to drive with a modicum of open road around you.

Satellite navigation systems are hot property, whether included as part of the car's specification or bought as an aftermarket extra. The built-in GPS systems on smartphones also work well. They're incredibly useful, but it's important to wear your caravanning hat when programming a route into a sat-nav console. The following cautionary tale was brought to my attention – and I don't imagine it's an isolated case.

Case study

'My second-hand Vauxhall Vectra came with a factory-fitted satellite navigation system, and my wife and I were just bowled over by it – we couldn't believe how clever it was. We would input a route into it, even if it was a journey we knew well – just for the novelty of it.

'Before we set off on our caravan holiday to a favourite site on the edge of Dartmoor in Devon, we keyed in the address and let the system guide us all the way.

'We weren't far away from the site when it gave us an instruction to turn off the main drag and join a minor road. I duly turned off ... and quickly realized what a big mistake that was. Within half a mile, the road began to climb steeply and it narrowed to a single track, hemmed in on both sides by high hedges.

'It was a nightmare. Cars coming in the opposite direction had to reverse back up the hill until they could squeeze into a side turning to let me pass. Some of the looks I was getting ...

'I had to do so many hill starts, I could smell the clutch overheating and was worried sick that it would burn out. I could see from the sat-nav that a "proper" road wasn't far away, and I have never been so relieved in my life to reach it.

'Since then, I've been wary of being guided on to minor roads when towing the caravan – especially in hilly areas.'

Doug, Bedfordshire

Remember this

Sat-navs are great – I wouldn't be without mine. But I always make sure I have a good road atlas to hand as well. Not only does it help avoid what happened to Doug, but it's a big help to have one in the caravan when planning days out or looking for ideas of where to go.

STAY LOCAL – DON'T OVERDO IT

'Stay local' doesn't mean booking into the site down the road from your house for a two-week holiday; it means stay local when you get where you're going to, whether that's 20 miles from your front door or 200 miles.

When you're finding out about things to do and places to see after you've arrived on site, try to limit yourself to those 'must see' attractions that are within a relaxed travelling distance of your temporary home base. That theme park may look delightfully nearby on the map, but if you have to drive through three busy town centres to get there and then 30 miles on an A-road with not a single overtaking opportunity, you'll be frazzled by the time you get there two hours later and, caught up in afternoon rush-hour traffic, even more frazzled when you get back.

Don't be over-ambitious. Remember, you're on holiday – so why spend much of it stuck in traffic? If you really, really want to visit that theme park, leave it until next time, when you can book into a good site that's a lot closer.

When you're booking the site, take advantage of local knowledge and ask the person on the other end of the phone about attractions nearby. Recommended walks? Good cycle rides? Safe beach for swimming? You can then follow up any good pointers by doing your own research.

WHEN ARE YOU GOING TO GO?

Every caravan owner in the country, it seems, goes caravanning at Bank Holiday weekends. I would like to suggest that, for this very reason, you buck the trend by doing precisely the opposite and staying at home. Sites are full to bursting and so are roads and visitor attractions. Unless there's a compelling reason for setting off somewhere in the caravan just because you have one extra day's break, don't do it.

Easter traditionally heralds the start of the caravanning season; if you want to stand even a chance of finding a pitch on a popular site, you will need to book early. The same applies during the extended school summer holidays when, for obvious reasons, sites both in the UK and overseas are busy for weeks on end.

If you're caravanning with your school-age children, you have little choice but to book your holidays out of term time. If that particular responsibility doesn't apply to you, take full advantage. If nothing else, site fees will be much cheaper – but there are other compelling reasons. You'll find that the warden and his or her team, no longer run off their feet, will have more time to stop and pass the time of day with you. You may even be able to choose your own pitch. Everything will just have a far more relaxed ambience.

To say that caravanning is a broad church would be putting it mildly. So, if your personal preference is for a holiday in a child-free environment, there are adult-only sites that cater for this, meaning you can still enjoy a break in mid-August and not encounter a bouncing ball, scooter or BMX bike the whole time you're there. There are also sites that don't allow dogs. Although, as far as I'm aware, there aren't any sites that allow neither children nor dogs.

Remember this

Caravanning with children? From personal experience, I would suggest that the quality of a caravan site's play area is of considerable importance. Sometimes, it's nice just to be able to sit and read the paper or sift through some local attraction leaflets for 20 minutes after clearing the breakfast things away – and if there's somewhere decent for the kids to pass the time before you go out for the day, it's a huge help.

It also keeps those 'When can we go? I'm bored' or 'Is tea nearly ready?' interjections to a minimum. A site with a play area and a grassy field to kick a ball around in? A desirable combination indeed ...

Key point

Write down your caravan's vital statistics – overall height and overall width, in both metric and imperial measurements – on a slip of paper or on the back of a business card and leave it in the glovebox or behind your sun visor.

If you encounter a road sign warning of maximum height or width restrictions, you will then be able to find out quickly whether or not you need to take the alternative route. Having this information immediately to hand is also handy for car parks, some of which have height restrictions intended to debar lorries or coaches, but which are perfectly okay for caravans.

If you add a roof-mounted aerial, don't forget to take account of the extra height – or there'll be no telly for you for a couple of weeks.

Best of Blighty – touring in the UK

Caravanning is popular nearly everywhere in Europe and so it's a continent that is spectacularly well set up to cater for its millions of participants. That includes the UK, of course, where it would be perfectly possible for you to buy a caravan tomorrow and take it somewhere different every day. Only if you're a sprightly young thing would you need to stay at the same site twice, and that would be some decades down the line.

Remember this

If you're holidaying in the British Isles (especially in the upland areas – Wales, the Lake District, the Scottish Highlands), you need to adopt a wholly positive attitude towards the weather, i.e. 'There's no such thing as poor weather, only poor clothing.' Regardless of the time of year, reserve a corner of the car boot for your waterproofs – and always, always pack wellies for the kids. Then you can get out and do stuff, letting the weather do its worst.

There isn't anywhere on the British mainland (or the majority of its islands) beyond the reach of your caravan. So, where are the places to head for? The following whistle-stop tour is based on a combination of great regions to go touring in and my personal knowledge that there are superb caravan sites to take advantage of.

DEVON AND CORNWALL

It's no coincidence that our tour begins in the south-west corner of England. Between them, these two counties are the most popular caravanning destinations – as anyone who has ever travelled south on the M5 on the first Saturday of the summer holidays can readily confirm.

It's not just caravanners who flock here in high numbers; holidaymakers of all persuasions are attracted and then seduced by the many scenic treasures that Devon and Cornwall have to offer.

With 360 miles of coastline – the longest of any county in England – Cornwall offers seaside holidays of every shape and colour, and some of Britain's best caravan sites have emerged here to meet the huge demand. Some of the bigger holiday parks are eye-wateringly expensive in high season, but a large proportion of the cost of a pitch on such sites goes towards paying for the on-site amenities, which may extend to indoor and outdoor swimming pools, giant water slides, evening entertainment, bars and restaurants.

If you don't intend to take advantage of any or most of these, it's better to save some money and choose a more low-key site that may still have worthwhile facilities such as a nice little bar and a decent restaurant, but without all the attached bells and whistles. There are plenty of such sites in Cornwall.

Some of the Cornish coastal sites offer views to die for. I know of one caravanning family that came across such a site while on holiday a long time ago – and they now never go anywhere else. They spend every summer there, and rarely – if ever – use the car once they've arrived because the dramatic coastline on the doorstep allows them to fill their days with beachcombing, cycling, picnicking and reacquainting themselves with the dozens of favourite seaside walks they've discovered over the years.

Generally speaking, north Cornwall is lined by impressive cliffs, which form a protective background to loads of great beaches. You get an altogether different experience on the south coast, which is more gentle, with rolling hills and fields, and pretty-as-a-picture bays.

Although this area is packed with holidaymakers at the height of the summer, there are enough beaches away from the busier resorts to give you the space to enjoy them.

The entire coastline of both counties comprises a major section of the South West Coast Path, the 630-mile waymarked trail that's one of the jewels in the crown of Britain's long-distance footpaths. If you're caravanning anywhere near the coast in either Devon or Cornwall, you are – by definition – within easy reach of a stretch of it. Commit to doing all of it by all means – but using your caravan as a base is a great way to enjoy walking different sections of it.

It's not just the coast that makes this part of the world so special, though. Dartmoor is a good enough reason in its own right to take a holiday here. The remotest, bleakest parts of this 350-square-mile national park in south Devon make you feel as though you're on the very edge of the world ... but in reality you're probably not very far from one of Dartmoor's impossibly pretty villages that looks like something out of a film set.

Choose your caravan site well when booking your fortnight's holiday, and you can spend one week using it as a base from which to explore this exceptional natural treasure (horse riders, mountain bikers, walkers and lovers of terrific country inns are all well catered for) and as a base from which to 'do' the south Devon coast the other week.

Key point

Don't underestimate the amount of time it'll take you to travel to Cornwall (assuming you don't already live in the south-west), especially in high season. The M5 can resemble a 50-mile-long car park when it's at its worst, and the A30, which the M5 funnels into, is one of Britain's most congested trunk roads.

One way to avoid all this is to plan to drive through the night so that you arrive at your chosen site in the morning – having confirmed that the owners are happy for you to arrive at an earlier than usual hour. Nobody in your household will thank you at the time for making them forsake a nice, warm bed for a seat in a car at such an ungodly hour ... but they will when they hear the horror stories on local radio traffic bulletins as you hand out the first bacon rolls of the holiday.

THE COTSWOLDS

This is, and always will be, one of my very favourite touring destinations. It covers a huge area, taking in bits of six counties in the heart of England. It has been designated an 'area of outstanding natural beauty' (the largest in England and Wales), a description it merits several times over. If you're intent on using your caravan to make the most of what the British countryside has to offer, you just can't improve on the Cotswolds.

Certainly, the main towns in the area, such as Stow-on-the-Wold, Broadway and Cirencester, can be devilishly busy, but head for the (ever so gentle) hills and prepare to be captivated by a landscape that seems almost frozen in time. You could be forgiven for thinking that you simply don't get countryside like this in Britain any more... but here it is in all its pastoral magnificence. And the Cotswold villages, complete with trademark honey-coloured limestone buildings, are just as easy on the eye as their natural surroundings.

Take your pick from the entire repertoire of caravan sites: everything from hidden-away, £4-a-night farm sites to full-on holiday parks with bars, shops and fitness centres await you in the Cotswolds. It's easy to go touring here too – the whole region is framed by the M4, M5 and M40 motorways, and the roads that criss-cross its finely-honed features are almost all ideally suited for towing.

WALES

Many of the best Welsh caravan sites are, unsurprisingly, to be found in and around Snowdonia. In this part of north Wales there's far more to get excited about than the mountain – the highest in England and Wales – that gives its name to the region.

For example, if the idea of taking cycling holidays in your caravan appeals, this is a dream destination. There are literally hundreds of miles of mountain bike tracks and trails that wend their way through the huge expanses of forest that cluster around the mountains. Some – the most prominent of which is Coed-y-Brenin – are part of dedicated mountain bike centres, where waymarked routes cater for riders of all capabilities. You don't need to have a head for heights to enjoy walking in Snowdonia, either. At any of the sites you book into, you'll be able to pick up information about the family-friendly, low-level walks that allow you to see this spectacular area at its best.

Snowdon itself is extremely accessible. You can walk to the summit if you're so inclined, or you can enjoy the singular pleasure of reaching it courtesy of the Snowdon Mountain Railway, often included in travel writers' lists of the world's great railway journeys. It climbs more than 915 metres in under five miles as it makes its way from the start in Llanberis to within a few feet of the summit. The crumbling old café on the summit, which Prince Charles described memorably as 'Britain's highest slum', was replaced in 2009 by a brand-new building that has generated rather more favourable reviews.

As with all the areas that come under the spotlight here, there are plenty of caravan sites – some with suitably commanding views of the towering mountains.

If you really want to get away from it all, caravanners are well catered for on the Lleyn Peninsula, Snowdonia's next-door neighbour. (One of the most popular sites in the Camping and Caravanning Club's network is in the village of Llanystumdwy, which is easier to get to than it is to pronounce.)

Lleyn, which forms the northern boundary of Cardigan Bay, is beautifully remote – with the accent on the beautiful and on the remote. Lovely beaches and sheltered bays vie for your attention with quaint fishing villages and views of the mountains, which begin their domination of the scenery very near to the coastline.

If you feel especially in need of a bit of personal battery-charging, Lleyn will suit you perfectly – and its fine roads are great for the caravan.

The other part of Wales I would choose to single out is Pembrokeshire – at the southern extremity of Cardigan Bay. It's quite a trek to get there for many visitors, but the effort is worth it. The coastal scenery here is some of the most dramatic you'll find anywhere in the British Isles, and the Pembrokeshire Coast Path takes you right into the heart of the action; it seems that each rise you crest rewards you with a vista even more unbelievable than the one you've just been stunned by.

Most of the 186-mile-long path lies within the boundary of the Pembrokeshire Coast National Park. It's one of those places where, if the weather's kind, you wouldn't want to be anywhere else. There are some sections where you can walk for hours without seeing another soul, and there are some first-class caravan sites to use as your base(s). If you don't mind basic facilities, you can extend your choice to dozens of smaller, quieter sites, many of them with exceedingly pretty outlooks.

THE SCOTTISH HIGHLANDS

'I never knew there was so much of it' is not an unusual comment from first-time visitors to the two-thirds of the Scottish mainland that make up Europe's last great wilderness. Average driving speeds are low but, for the most part, you wouldn't want it to be any other way for fear of missing any of the natural splendour surrounding you.

Some caravanners are put off touring in the Highlands because of the perceived difficulty of towing on the single-track roads that are commonplace there. This is an own goal of epic proportions.

In fact, towing a caravan on single-track roads is delightfully straightforward. The passing places aren't solely for giving way to traffic coming in the opposite direction, they should also be used to let following traffic past – regardless of whether you're towing a caravan or not (see Figure 9.1).

In practice, towing on single-track roads adds little or nothing to journey times compared to travelling in a solo vehicle. Before long, you will acquire the knack of indicating left, slowing down and letting the vehicle behind scoot past. You'll invariably

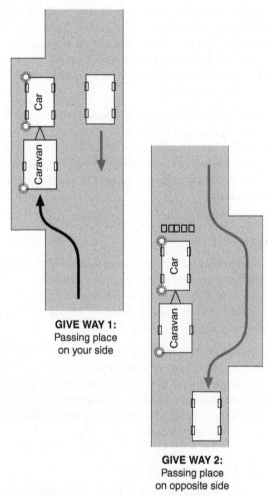

GIVE WAY 1:
Passing place
on your side

GIVE WAY 2:
Passing place
on opposite side

Figure 9.1 Passing places – remember to use your indicators.

get a wave or a 'toot' of thanks and be back on your way without actually having had to stop at all.

If the next passing place is on your offside (i.e. on the right-hand side), just slow down or stop adjacent to it and let the vehicle behind pass you by using the passing place. Just be aware that some drivers – often, though not always, overseas visitors – will veer over into the passing place on the opposite side, perhaps caught out by not having encountered any oncoming traffic for miles.

Wester Ross, the Ardnamurchan peninsula, the Isle of Skye (the beautiful bridge connecting it to the mainland is now toll-free), Royal Deeside, Argyll … the list of Highland areas that you will look forward to visiting again is a long one. And rest assured that the quality of caravan sites in the far north is as good as anywhere.

Key point

Although the much-reviled Highland midges aren't as omnipresent as some people would have you believe, they can be a problem in some areas in summer, so it pays to go armed with some spray repellent for when you're out and about. A bespoke candle or lamp for balmy evenings in the awning may also end up paying its way.

If your caravan doesn't have flyscreens fitted to at least some of its opening windows, this is an upgrade well worth considering. Whether in the Highlands or elsewhere in summer, you daren't open any unprotected doors or windows after dusk, especially with the lights on, if you don't want to be pestered by insect intruders. Some caravans have flyscreens that pull across to protect the door as well.

BRITAIN OFF THE BEATEN TRACK
There are some wonderful corners of the UK ready for you to explore – places that hide their light under a bushel, but which are well worth a visit.

A case in point is rural Northumberland, a vast hinterland of charming, sturdy villages, wide-open moorland and a fabulously unspoiled coastline. All most people see of it is a token glimpse as they motor up or down the A1 on their way to somewhere else. Make that detour.

If you follow the A1 into Scotland, you'll be on one of the very few busy roads that run through the Scottish Borders. The entire area between the A74 in the west and the A1 in the east boasts one of the lowest population densities in the UK and some of the finest scenery.

The hills may not be as mighty as those in the Highlands, but they have a drama and a charm all of their own, and handsome towns and villages such as Moffat, Jedburgh, Melrose, Yetholm and Selkirk make fine touring bases.

There aren't any very high hills in Lincolnshire, but the Wolds are serenely beautiful and an area served by some cracking caravan sites. From here, you can strike out to the seaside for the singularly bracing experience of a stay on the Lincolnshire coast. Sutton-on-Sea is delightfully laid-back – and there's a good Caravan Club site there.

There's plenty of good accommodation to be found in south Shropshire, a personal favourite. This, too, is a big, uncrowded county with plenty of surprises in store for anyone who's never been. The area around Church Stretton in the Shropshire Hills is known locally as Little Switzerland, and with good reason – there are definite Alpine tendencies to the beautiful surroundings.

There are plenty of superb country inns and pubs in these parts, with a plethora of great walks and bike rides to take advantage of.

I could go on: East Kent, inland Norfolk, Wiltshire, Fife … Where shall we go next, indeed. It's a fine conundrum to be faced with.

Meeting up with others

If the idea of caravanning with a group of like-minded friends appeals, there's a wide-ranging social network for you to take advantage of. If you become a member of either of the major clubs – the Caravan Club or the Camping and Caravanning Club – you're automatically entitled to attend the hundreds of rallies and other get-togethers that are organized by the members themselves at a local level.

It can be a good way to make new friends very quickly, not to mention getting to see some parts of the country you may not otherwise have gone to and tapping into decades' worth of caravanning experience gathered together on one rally field.

The Camping and Caravanning Club also has 'special interest sections', where members with a particular passion for such activities as photography, canoeing or folk singing meet up to indulge themselves in their chosen pastime.

There are lots of other caravanning clubs that may appeal to you. Most of the major marques have dedicated owners' clubs, run by enthusiastic owners but with close links to the manufacturers who can see the commercial sense in being nice to people with such brand loyalty.

You could easily find yourself with a bulging social calendar if you start attending rallies and other weekend activities. But you won't get the hard-sell to be an active, participating member if you join one of the major clubs; the majority of their members are perfectly happy just to do their own thing and enjoy caravanning their own way.

Key point

If you like the idea of meeting up with other caravanners at rallies, bear in mind that these usually take place on a friendly landowner's field or some other rural land devoid of the amenities you usually expect to see on a 'normal' caravan site. The invitations to attend these events in the clubs' respective magazines will make this clear by using the description 'own san ess'. It stands for 'own sanitation essential', meaning there's no shower block or toilet, so make sure you come suitably provided for.

Most modern caravans will be perfectly well-equipped to see you through a long weekend like this, but you may care to consider caravans with more upmarket washroom facilities if you think there's a chance that you'll spend a lot of time on a rally field. Some cheaper or older caravans may have electric-only systems, which obviously won't be any use to you in a field without access to a mains hook-up.

The same caveat applies if you're going to be a relatively frequent user of the small Certificated Location or Certificated Site hideaways referred to in Chapter 6. A gas water-heater and a roomy shower cubicle separate from the toilet compartment will make life much, much more comfortable in such spartan surroundings.

All-year-round caravanning

It's still the case that most caravan sites are shut over the winter, but an increasing number are staying open for longer – and you won't have to search too hard to find sites that stay open all year round. You still need to search out quality, however. Are the site access roads and perimeter roads firm-surfaced for optimum traction in icy or snowy weather? Are the shower blocks centrally heated?

Most caravans, too, are well up to the task of keeping you warm and comfortable, even when winter's doing its worst. Those models with a combined gas/electric heater make the better year-round tourers. Depending on the weather, you may find that you need to have the heater on all the time – even through the night – to maintain a comfortable temperature. If you were to do so with your heater solely on the gas setting, you would use up your supplies of LPG quicker than you would probably like.

So, run the heater on electricity. You pay a flat nightly fee for the hook-up facility, regardless of how much power you use, so one way of looking at it is that you're effectively operating it for nothing – and conserving your gas supplies into the bargain.

From a safety point of view, use the heater on its electric setting if you want to leave it on overnight (which you probably will as an unheated caravan in winter quickly becomes nothing more than an oversized icebox). Although a regularly serviced caravan gas system is safe and reliable, it relies on effective, unhindered ventilation.

In really cold weather, there's always the risk (however slight) of a severe overnight snowfall that could build up around and under the caravan, blocking off the floor-level ventilation holes. If your caravan's built-in space heater doesn't have an electric function, bring along a low-wattage fan heater and put that on a low setting overnight. If snow does fall and starts to lie thickly, keep the underside of the caravan clear of it and don't allow the roof-mounted flue to become blocked, either.

Don't be afraid to be nosy on site. Walk around and see how seasoned, all-year caravanning veterans survive – indeed, enjoy – the winter. You'll see small porch awnings, where muddy boots, wellies, brollies, waterproofs, hats and other paraphernalia can all be deposited before entering the cosy sanctuary of the caravan. You'll probably also see some wise owls who have laid some outdoor-type tiles (as used on patios or to surround outdoor swimming pools, for example) around the entrance step.

In freezing conditions, you'll see water pumps being disconnected and brought indoors last thing at night (and you might see that the water container, if that's not coming indoors as well, at least has a protective, insulated jacket enveloping it). You'll see kettles being filled up last thing at night, just in case – despite all the precautions – the water does freeze up. The smug kettle-fillers will still enjoy that important first cuppa in the morning.

Key point

There are two types of LPG (liquefied petroleum gas) you can use in your caravan – propane and butane. If you intend to carry on touring throughout the winter, make sure you're equipped with propane (which comes in red cylinders), because butane (blue cylinders) will cease to operate as the temperature drops to near freezing point.

Focus points

The main points to remember from this chapter are:

* When you own a caravan, one of the great pleasures after coming back from a trip is planning the next one.
* Make the journey part of the holiday if you can. Plan a nice route ...
* ... but double-check sat nav instructions on a map. Not every road is suitable for a car and caravan.
* If you're able to avoid Bank Holidays and school holidays, do so. Sites and attractions are at their busiest and prices will invariably be higher.
* Beautiful Devon and Cornwall understandably attract thousands of holidaymakers in peak season. Consider travelling through the night to avoid the worst of the inevitable traffic congestion.
* For a multi-activity holiday, Snowdonia is hard to beat: opportunities for walking, climbing, mountain-biking and scenic drives are top-drawer – and a caravan makes a perfect base.
* The Scottish Highlands is another fantastic caravanning destination. Frequent passing places make towing on single-track roads very straightforward.
* Use the caravan to its full potential by exploring parts of the country you've never been to before.
* If you really get the caravanning bug and want to meet up with like-minded enthusiasts, join a caravanning club and take advantage of the many rallies and other social get-togethers on offer.
* Caravanning in winter can be fun. Wrap up warm and give it a try ...

10

What it's all about – the joys of touring overseas

In this chapter, you will learn:

▶ *all about planning and booking your first foreign caravanning trip*

▶ *ideas for holidays in France, Spain and other continental destinations*

▶ *how to spend the winter in warmer climes.*

Many caravanners are perfectly happy to confine their touring exclusively to the British mainland – and as we saw in Chapter 9 they're spoiled for choice.

With or without a caravan, though, an overseas holiday adds a big helping of extra excitement. And you only need to drive through the first village after disembarking the ferry at Calais to realize that a continental tour offers a different experience altogether.

Continental Europe is, if anything, even better disposed towards camping and caravanning than the UK. Whereas caravanning is still regarded by some observers in Britain as just a bit twee, there are no such reservations on the continent. There, a caravan is seen as nothing more than a holiday on wheels, and my experience is that, in general, there's a greater tolerance of caravans from other road users. I once got lost trying to find our overnight-stop caravan site in Zaragoza in northern Spain and ended up mixing it with the teatime rush-hour traffic in the city-centre streets. If that had been Manchester or Edinburgh, I'd no doubt have had to endure some icy stares and angrily flashed headlights. By contrast, the Spanish drivers didn't bat a collective eyelid and were impressively courteous as I eventually made my way out to the sanctuary of the ring road.

Key point

Arm yourself with detailed directions for each site you're visiting. This is especially important when touring overseas, where you have to concentrate additionally on driving on the right and dealing with signposts to places that will be unfamiliar to you.

Many sites will have their own websites from which you can download or copy directions, or you can ask the owner to email you the best route, taking account of local landmarks such as filling stations or prominent buildings. As in the UK, Google's excellent Streetview function can be really helpful.

If you're investing in a foreign sites guide – highly recommended if you're touring from place to place – make sure you choose one that features regularly updated reviews based on actual site visits and includes directions to each establishment listed.

It's impossible to generalize about the quality of continental sites compared to their British equivalents. Just like in the UK, they vary tremendously in size, facilities offered and quality. Pitches are often smaller, so you must make sure you can be accommodated if you're touring with an especially large caravan.

You may also find that the amperage of the electric hook-up facility is lower than in the UK, meaning that you will need to exercise some restraint in using appliances on board to avoid 'tripping' the electricity supply to you and your neighbours. In practice, it's not a huge problem: it probably means nothing more than waiting until you've finished with the hairdryer before you switch the kettle on.

Many of the overseas sites used by British-based holiday operators (including both the major clubs and Eurocamp) will give little flavour of being in a foreign land. During the summer holidays, a big percentage of those staying there will be from Britain, so you'll have little opportunity to practise your foreign language skills on-site.

Your first foreign caravanning holiday

The internet has radically transformed the way we plan and book our holidays, whether it's sorting out flights, a villa and car hire for a couple of weeks in Majorca or organizing a caravan holiday on the French Atlantic coast.

If you've read about a particular caravan site – maybe via a travel feature in one of the caravanning magazines, inclusion in a holiday brochure or a listing in a continental sites guide – a quick online search will more than likely result in relevant links to all manner of websites. These may include: caravanning forums where holidaymakers who have already been there will give you their views on the place; camping and caravanning site listings for particular areas (giving you the wherewithal to check out other possibilities); plus, of course, the website of the establishment itself.

The seemingly omnipresent TripAdvisor website also covers caravan sites.

If you call up Google or some other search engine and enter the name of a site you're considering for a family holiday in France, you may be rewarded by an all-encompassing official website that includes 360-degree panoramic views of the restaurant, bar, swimming pool complex and private beach. That will give you the confidence to go ahead and book it.

RESERVING YOUR PITCH

There are two ways to go about this. You can contact the site directly by phone or email or, if it's on the books of one of the British-based foreign travel service providers, you can leave everything to them. Do note, though, that in order to take advantage of the overseas travel services operated by the Caravan Club or the Camping and Caravanning Club, you'll need to be a member. There are independent operators available as well.

Using one of the specialist providers to obtain an inclusive package that encompasses a ferry or Channel Tunnel crossing, any stopover sites and the required number of nights at your main destination, does have its advantages.

Foremost is the fact that one phone conversation will sort everything. Those operators have 'real-time' access to all the cross-Channel providers' schedules and bookings, so they can check availability on your preferred crossings while you chat to them. They're also often able to secure the most competitive prices, due to the 'clout' that they carry with the site owners and ferry/tunnel operators.

Remember this

It pays to be decisive when you're booking overseas sites and/or Channel crossings, especially in peak season. If you think about it too long, you'll lose out. It's happened to me before. For sea crossings, the problem is exacerbated when a caravan comes into the equation, because operators allocate only so much deck space to vehicles with trailers – and when they're gone, that's it.

Case study: why overseas motoring cover is a good idea

Never venture overseas without making sure you have all-encompassing breakdown and recovery cover in place for both the car and the caravan. Terry and Ann Sinclair, from Doncaster, South Yorkshire, are certainly glad they did.

'We had to be recovered from northern Spain back to the UK when our car – which was only a few months old at the time – developed a fault that couldn't be fixed locally.

'Luckily, we had taken out the requisite level of cover through the club we had booked the holiday with. Not only were all the arrangements taken care of in Spain and in the UK, but the modest fee I'd paid prevented a bill that would have run easily into four figures.

'It wasn't quite the end to the holiday we'd have planned, but we could at least relax in the knowledge that we'd get home safely.'

How to get there

Far and away the most popular option among caravanners is to take the short-hop Channel crossing via either the 'Chunnel', from just outside Folkestone to Calais, or the Dover–Calais ferry.

The road network around Calais has been comprehensively upgraded over the past few years and you'll soon be speeding on your way on fast, high-quality autoroutes in whichever direction you need to go.

But there are other options:

▶ If you're heading to the south of France or Spain, long-haul sea crossings from Plymouth to Santander and from Portsmouth to Bilbao or Santander will cut out a massive amount of road miles.

▶ Portsmouth also serves as the main departure point for ferries sailing directly to Normandy – to Le Havre, Caen, St Malo and Cherbourg. The south-coast ports of Weymouth and Poole also offer sailings to this part of France.

► If you're heading to Scandinavia, ships sail from the Essex port of Harwich to Esbjerg on the Danish Jutland peninsula. From Newcastle, you can sail directly to Amsterdam.

What's the better bet for those heading south towards the Vendée, Bordeaux, Biarritz and destinations in Spain? Drive or long-haul ferry crossing? There are pros and cons for either option. Let's consider the long sea crossing first.

Pros:

► These mighty sea crossings are akin to mini-cruises and are a great way to really kick-start your holiday. Facilities on board include a choice of bars and restaurants, cinemas, fitness rooms, cabaret and other evening entertainment.

► If you have had to drive a considerable distance from your home just to reach Portsmouth or Plymouth, you'll probably be very glad of the opportunity to leave the car and caravan below decks for one or two nights and enjoy the chance to sit back and have a few drinks in the bar while the nautical miles pass by.

► You'll arrive in Spain refreshed and raring to go. It's a very satisfying feeling to roll on to Spanish soil, knowing that you haven't driven a mile since you left the UK.

► The Bay of Biscay is a veritable treasure chest of marine life. Keen naturalists travel on the ferries purely to spot the whales and dolphins – sightings of which are the rule rather than the exception. The thrill of seeing a huge fin whale and her pup just metres from the ship is one I'll never forget.

Cons:

► The long-haul crossings to northern Spain are very, very expensive for a car and caravan combination, especially in high season. You'll also need to make your booking really early, as places for larger vehicles are restricted. You'll be fortunate indeed to be able to book a summer voyage in February.

► The Bay of Biscay has a reputation for being rough, so sufferers of sea-sickness may choose to steer clear. Having said that, I've made this crossing six times and have yet to experience anything that could be described as dramatic.

▶ Nobody likes to start off their holiday by counting the pennies, but the food on the ferry can be expensive. Take as much on board with you as you can – biscuits, crisps, fruit, bottled water and so on – to keep the expense to a minimum.

Remember this

When you're loading up the car, try to have your 'ship bags' ready-packed for taking on board – it can be a nightmare rummaging around for a misplaced iPod in the dark, cramped confines of a car deck. Make sure you've got everything, because you won't be allowed back on to the car deck once the voyage is under way. Always carry your passports with you. And always make a note of exactly where on the car deck you are – if you're very late in finding your car at disembarkation time and delay the vehicles stacked up behind you, you'll have to run the gauntlet of disapproving stares.

France

Towing speed limit

▶ 90 kph (56 mph) on single-carriageway roads outside built-up areas (80 kph/50 mph in bad weather).

▶ 110–130 kph (68–81 mph) on motorways (110 kph/68 mph in bad weather).

Mandatory equipment

▶ Warning triangle, spare bulbs, breathalyser kit, hi-viz vest (carry one for each occupant).

Have a look at a map of France and you can see at a glance what makes it such a magnificent destination for a touring holiday. It's an enormous country – only Russia and Ukraine in Europe are bigger – yet its population is similar to that of the overcrowded UK. Furthermore, with a road network that is simply staggering, you can travel in splendid isolation for day after day – although it's a different story in and around the bigger towns, cities and resorts.

If you want to get somewhere quickly in France, you'll find that the autoroutes are reliably free-flowing, and often devoid of traffic to the extent that it's something of a culture shock to anyone familiar with the congested British motorway network. Most autoroutes are *péage* (toll) roads, and you can spend a small fortune if you're travelling a long distance, but the ease with which miles are eaten up – especially when towing – makes this, to my mind, something worth paying for. I heartily recommend the excellent www.autoroutes.fr website, where you can (in English) plan a route and at the same time see how much it'll cost you in tolls and fuel.

Autoroutes are also serviced at regular intervals by *aires*, which the French are justly proud of. These are rest areas, with plenty of dedicated parking spaces for cars with caravans. Facilities typically consist of a toilet, telephone, picnic tables and perhaps a modest play area for children.

They're great places to stop for a rest or a picnic lunch if you don't need fuel or any of the other facilities of a big service area, but you emphatically should not be tempted to stay overnight in an *aire*. There have been isolated reports of overnighting caravanners and motorcaravanners being targeted by thieves in *aires*, so please always take advantage of the security of a registered site.

France is an overwhelmingly safe destination for British holidaymakers and *aires* are perfectly fine to use in the daytime, when there will most likely be plenty of other motorists using them.

Remember this

Great though the French autoroutes are, all the swift progress you've been making can suddenly come to nothing if you encounter a queue for the tolls (*péage*). They can be lengthy affairs on certain roads at certain times – on the autoroutes heading towards Calais on a Sunday afternoon, for example – which may leave you anxiously looking at the clock if you have a ferry to catch. Always build in plenty of time to your journey calculations to take account of this. If you encounter long queues at the toll plaza, you'll usually find that the queues for the credit card payment booths are much shorter.

Away from the autoroutes, N-class roads (Routes Nationales) are the equivalent of British A-roads; you'll often find an N-road shadowing an autoroute, giving a toll-free alternative. If you're not in any particular hurry and/or have an aversion to paying tolls, you should usually be able to plot a viable route to your destination. Even more minor roads are often perfectly fine for towing a caravan on.

As in the UK, fuel prices are quite a bit more expensive at motorway service areas than elsewhere locally, so avoid filling up at these outlets whenever possible.

Key point

There's no shortage of good-quality road atlases and map sheets covering the vast French road network. Equip yourself with a large-scale version to take the fullest advantage of the plethora of options open to you when touring, with or without the caravan. Michelin maps have a particularly desirable feature, shading especially scenic routes in green. This is highly useful when planning day trips from a site or detours away from the monotony of the autoroute. If you own a sat nav unit, you can buy mapping software for most European countries if you don't already have it.

If you're driving through France in the middle of the day, away from the 24-hour service areas of the autoroutes, make sure you have plenty of fuel in your tank – not to mention supplies for lunch, if you're planning on having a picnic. It's not a myth that France effectively comes to a grinding halt for two hours or more around lunchtime; it's really true. Shops, offices – and filling stations – close their doors while staff head off to take advantage of the *menu du jour* at local restaurants and, if you're away from the bigger centres of population, you may have difficulty finding a petrol station that's open.

Indeed, filling stations can be thin on the ground in France in any case, so always take advantage of any opportunity to fill up if your fuel gauge is showing less than half-full and you still have a fair amount of mileage to cover. Some stations have automated pumps that allow you to pay by credit card, but it's risky to assume you'll always be able to do so in your moment of need.

And don't forget – always take advantage of fuel/rest stops to check the integrity of your outfit: electrical cables not dangling too near the ground; jockey wheel clamp still good and tight; nothing rolling about inside the caravan that might cause damage.

Navigating your way out of towns and villages in France can sometimes catch you off guard, with several different turnings often radiating out from town squares. The best advice is always to know the names of the roads you want to take, rather than just the names of the towns you want to be driving towards.

Sometimes, you'll look at a map and quite understandably pick out Town A and Town B as the places to look for on the signposts. This doesn't always work, as you may find that Town C will be on there as well as a couple of villages, the names of which you didn't notice on the map. However, French signposts always give the road numbers – so that's the most reliable thing to look out for, above all else.

Similarly, every town and village has a nameplate at its end, giving you a chance to plot your position on the map if you happened to miss the name of the town on the way in. It also confirms the number of the road you're driving on, a superb example of logical thinking that makes life much easier by preventing you from driving too far down the wrong road before realizing your mistake and having to turn around.

Important – Know your priorities

Many British motorists get caught unawares by the French rule of giving priority to traffic coming from the right, even if that road is obviously a minor route exiting on to a more prominent thoroughfare. Just to make matters more complicated, it's not a universal edict.

So if there are no road markings evident, the only safe option is to assume that anything coming from the right, especially in built-up areas, will have priority over you. Be prepared to give way. Sometimes, you will be able to see quite clearly that the turning on your right has a solid white stop line or give-way lines, in which case you clearly have priority.

Obviously, there's even more of a need for caravanners to exercise caution at such junctions, bearing in mind the length of the outfit and therefore the greater difficulty for a local driver of taking avoiding action if you inadvertently fail to give way to him or her. If in doubt, you've nothing to lose and everything to gain by slowing right down and preparing to give way, accelerating only when you're satisfied that the coast is clear.

WHERE TO GO

France is more akin to a small, self-contained continent than a country. It's an endlessly fascinating place, no matter how many times you visit, and there are always new delights to discover. Whether it's the breathtaking gorges and verdant hillsides of Provence, the seemingly endless beaches of the Atlantic coast, the sweeping, pastoral plains of Picardy, the tranquil remoteness of Burgundy, the almost Cornish ruggedness of the Brittany coastline or the awe-inspiring Alps and Pyrénées ... it's a dream destination for those of us who like to tour.

Even the caravan sites can yield a few surprises. There's one particular organization, Les Castels, which operates a network of more than 40 sites in some of the most idyllic locations across France, all situated in the grounds of magnificent châteaux and manor houses.

At some, you can book dinner in the château itself, with the owner as your host. When I did so a few years ago, my fellow diners and I were treated to a rousing solo performance on the French horn from the owner. Memorable to say the least, just like the wonderful site – complete with swimming pool in the formal gardens and a bar in a stylishly converted barn – in the midst of the Norman countryside.

Indeed, Normandy is an especially appealing destination for British caravanners, given the relative ease of getting there. Ferries sail from Portsmouth to Cherbourg, Le Havre and St Malo. The last-named – actually just over the border in neighbouring Brittany – boasts a terrific old walled town, within the confines of which are dozens of restaurants and bars. Many of them are unashamedly aimed at British holidaymakers, but that doesn't detract from the appeal of having an al fresco meal in such special surroundings.

The Normandy hinterland is a beguiling concoction of verdant, rolling countryside, charming villages and ancient towns such as Bayeux – home of the famous tapestry – and Honfleur, the almost unbelievably picturesque fishing village that has always attracted artists and their easels because of the lucid quality of the natural light.

Of course, there are miles of beaches – some of which will forever be remembered as the sites of the D-Day landings and which still have an evocative aura about them. There are also many museums in the area that commemorate the historic events of June 1944.

Because so many Channel ports are clustered around here, there are lots of good caravan sites within easy striking distance of them. Many caravanners plan their holidays so that they can enjoy two or three days in Normandy before catching the boat back home. There's so much to see and do in this one region alone, that it's become common for an one-night stopover to be quickly rebooked for a much longer stay.

If you continue to hug the Atlantic coast as you head south, you'll come to the distinctive peninsula that makes up Brittany. This part of France is massively popular with French holidaymakers as well as those from other countries, so it can be very busy in high season.

Most visitors tend to keep to the coast, and you can hardly blame them. Huge, expansive beaches, sheer cliffs, seductive bays, chocolate-box fishing villages with cute little restaurants hugging the shoreline ... Brittany is full of them.

The interior is much less crowded, even in summer, and makes a great destination for day-long cycle rides on the beguiling network of quiet country lanes, with perfect picnic spots seemingly lurking around every corner.

You may find more seclusion – not to mention unbroken sunshine – further south, either in the Vendée or Les Landes areas of the Atlantic coast. Both are well-served by caravan sites recommended by British travel operators and are within a day's drive of the Norman ports. If you're travelling from Calais, it's better to build in an overnight stop on the way.

The main attraction of many Vendée and Les Landes sites is their proximity to quite breathtaking beaches, some of which will have private access from the site itself. You don't need to be a beach bum to appreciate the beauty of the scenery on this stretch of coastline. If you enjoy swimming in the sea, the Atlantic coast has, in my opinion, much more to offer than the Mediterranean. It is often just as pleasantly warm but comes with the significant advantage of the never-ending Atlantic breakers that add a huge dose of fun to one's bathing exploits. Admittedly, if you have very young children, you may feel happier splashing about in the more benign Med.

The Vendée hinterland is actually very flat, to the great benefit of cyclists who like an easy time of it. The local authorities have gone to great lengths to provide mile after mile of dedicated cycle routes, all superbly signposted and almost all suitable for families.

Les Landes, south of the great Bordeaux vineyards, offers more stunning beaches, shallow lakes, hundreds of miles of woodland cycle rides/walks (take a map or, if you're showing off, a hand-held GPS system …), and one of Europe's most amazing natural phenomena, the colossal sand dune at Pyla, the biggest in the entire continent. Granted, you may use up a week's worth of energy climbing it, especially if you go down the other side to the beautiful beach – the only way out is all the way back up again. But this is not something you want to miss.

If the many delights of touring in your caravan to this part of the world – or anywhere else that enjoys sultry summer nights – are likely to draw you back, do make sure that you choose a caravan with flyscreens on at least some of the opening windows. And then, of course, ensure that it is those particular windows you open in the evening and during the night!

The last port of call on the French Atlantic coast is in the Pyrénées Atlantique département, with the twin attractions of those Atlantic breakers and, an easy day's drive from most of the holiday caravan sites along the coast, the mighty Pyrénées themselves. On a clear day, driving or walking in the higher reaches of these formidable mountains rewards you with views that are almost too stunning to comprehend. Sometimes, your vantage point will be so lofty that, instead of looking up to see eagles soaring, you look down on them.

By themselves, the Pyrénées are worth the long journey to the far south of France (or northern Spain). Stay on the coast – I've stayed on a fantasic beachside site in Bidart, just adjacent to charming Biarritz – and drive there on day trips, or choose a caravan site within sight of the foothills.

The other French holiday hotspot for caravanners is the Mediterranean coast in the south and south-east of the country, especially the Côte d'Azur. This isn't an expedition to be taken lightly, given the enormous distance involved in a return journey from the UK – but you can make the journey itself part of the adventure by researching interesting stopover locations on the way there and back.

For comfort, you should go for two in each direction. For example, an overnight halt in the Rhône valley will give you the satisfaction of having put a lot of miles behind you; and stopover number two could be at a site in the Provence hills. Although this isn't so far from the coast itself, it is a wonderful, life-affirming location in which to spend a few hours. The blend of craggy, unspoilt villages nestling prettily in the wooded hills, all accessed by first-class, well-surfaced roads, is too good to miss. The very fact that it'll take you just two or three hours to reach your final destination will give you a warm glow the next day, too.

The Côte d'Azur includes some of the most upmarket resorts in Europe, including Antibes and Juan les Pins, as well as the affluent city of Nice. Holiday accommodation in these parts can be costly – so it makes all the sense in the world to bring your own.

This corner of France is packed in high season so, if you want some respite from the continually busy beaches and promenades, the aforementioned Provence hills are but a short car ride away. Also, if you've never been to Italy before, the border is just along the road, giving you the opportunity to add it to your list of 'been there' countries.

For an altogether less busy French summer experience, stay away from the coast. Burgundy, in the east of the country, is a fine example as it has a delightfully off-the-beaten-track feel to it, even at the height of the holiday season. If that's high on your list of priorities, it's worth the full day's drive from Calais to get there. Good-quality caravan sites are plentiful, although they're less feature-packed than many of their brethren in the more obvious holiday hotspots.

The expansive Burgundian countryside is perfect for losing yourself in. Away from the busier N-roads, you can walk, cycle or drive for hours and never see another soul. When you do stop for a coffee and croissant in a village café, you may well be the only foreigners there. It's great for a holiday that allows you to sample something of the 'real' France.

Key point

If you have a long trip ahead of you to catch a ferry or a Channel Tunnel train, eradicate any prospect of missing it by checking into a site near the port/departure terminal the night before, leaving you with a relaxed journey of just a few miles the next day.

The last thing you need at either end of your holiday is the stress caused by an unforeseen hold-up – traffic accident, roadworks, taking a wrong turning – that may cause you to miss your crossing. Remember that your journey times with a car/caravan outfit will be slightly longer than with a solo car, so always plan accordingly.

Spain

Towing speed limit

▶ 70 kph (44 mph) on single-carriageway roads outside built-up areas.

▶ 80 kph (50 mph) on motorways.

Mandatory equipment

▶ Warning triangle (two recommended), spare bulbs, spare pairs of glasses for drivers who wear them, hi-viz vests (carry one for each occupant).

Be aware …

▶ Always turn on dipped headlights in tunnels, no matter how short.

If the very act of driving off the ferry in France already gives you the feeling of being somewhere 'foreign', the sense is heightened further when you arrive in Spain. The Spanish have a decidedly southern European approach to life that's far more laissez-faire than we're used to in the UK, an approach that's ideally suited to the caravanner seeking a relaxing, laid-back holiday.

For example, stroll into a restaurant in any Spanish town at 8 p.m. on a Saturday evening and you'll likely as not be dining by yourself. By 10 p.m. it's a different story. Entire families – grandparents and young children included – will be taking their places at table.

Whereas much of France comes to a halt for an extended lunch, much of Spain retreats indoors for an afternoon siesta. Both seem a million miles away from the typical British 'working lunch' of a sandwich hurriedly consumed at one's desk.

Just like its big neighbour to the north, Spain offers a dramatic variety of attractions to the visitor. If your preconceived notion when thinking of this country is of the Costa del Something-or-other, complete with faux Irish pubs and dreary little bars run by ex-pats that show *EastEnders* on giant-screen TVs every evening, you couldn't be more wide of the mark (even though such establishments do exist, admittedly).

Towering mountain ranges, sweeping plains, ancient hillside villages, some of the continent's most vibrant and cultured cities and every conceivable type of coastal scenery all await you.

Almost all of it is easily accessible for the touring caravanner, thanks to a national road network that has become one of the best in Europe, due in no small measure to an enormous injection of EU funds for road-building projects over the past couple of decades or so.

Most of the motorways (*autopistas*) are toll roads but, as in France, there are usually reasonably good-quality, toll-free alternatives following the same routes. Whichever road you choose, you have absolutely no excuse for running out of fuel in Spain; filling stations crop up everywhere, sometimes in the most remote, unlikely locations.

Key point

When choosing a caravan site in Spain, it's worth finding one with an on-site supermarket, because it will invariably be better-stocked than the one in the nearest town. There are exceptions, of course, but Spanish supermarkets are often small and carry a limited range of goods. The best on-site shops, however, cater for a cosmopolitan clientele – and you may find that you never need to stock up on provisions from anywhere else.

Spanish drivers don't have the best reputation for courteous driving, but they are – mostly – very accommodating to foreign motorists and are appreciative of the fact that you have a caravan in tow. Do what you can to maintain this level of understanding by pulling over to let local drivers past whenever possible.

WHERE TO GO

If you're travelling on one of the long-haul sailings to either Santander or Bilbao, you won't need to tow the caravan very far after you arrive to experience one of the nicest areas of the entire country – the Costa Verde, or Green Coast, so called because of its pleasantly verdant landscape.

The Costa Verde starts where the Bay of Biscay ends, encompassing the entire northern coastline. Fabulous beaches and pretty fishing villages often have a backdrop of densely wooded hills reminiscent of Alpine scenery, a paradise for walkers and mountain bikers. But the pièce de résistance in this corner of Spain is the Picos de Europa mountain range. Not as extensive or as high as the nearby Pyrénées perhaps, but every bit as awe-inspiring, with towering, jaggy peaks that can border on the intimidating.

Any of the fine caravan sites dotted along the coast make a great base for a day trip into the Picos. You may find that you want to leave the caravan behind for two or three days while you take time out to explore this magnificent area in more detail, taking advantage of B&B-type accommodation in the mountains. There's a bewildering network of high- and low-level walking and cycling trails to suit all abilities. If even the thought of that makes you feel slightly breathless, you can have the time of your life without leaving the car – there are plenty of fantastic drives to enjoy as well.

The Costa Blanca adds another day or two to your journey, taking a vaguely south-easterly route through Zaragoza (a recommended stopover) and the Rioja vineyards, past the sprawling metropolis of Barcelona.

You find amazing contrasts here. Many of the resorts and beaches are so busy that you can be forgiven for thinking that half of Europe has come on holiday to this part of the Mediterranean at the same time as you. Yet, pedal your bike for 15 minutes inland and you could be in a different country altogether. You can see the Med from some of the roads that meander up the hillsides, but you'll be the only one enjoying the view. Call into a village café for a drink, and you're likely to be the only non-local there.

Many of the resorts on the Costa Blanca are within easy reach of a railway station, all of which offer frequent services into nearby Barcelona. It's a marvellous city, with a real buzz about it – day and night.

If you don't mind a long-haul drive, Andalucia in the far south of the country is a fascinating holiday destination. As well as the old cities of Seville (there really are oranges everywhere ...) and Jerez, home of sherry, the countryside is big and open, endowing everywhere with a wonderful feeling of space.

This is also where you can take a day trip from Europe to Africa, thanks to frequent ferry crossings that make the short hop across the Mediterranean from the port of Algeciras to Tangier or Ceuta in Morocco.

Key point

If you're able to go touring on the continent away from the mad rush of high season, you can buy books of discounted pitch fee vouchers, called Camping Cheques or Touring Cheques, that are accepted at hundreds of sites across Europe. However, the Camping Cheque scheme offers a far greater reach, with more than 600 sites on its books compared to the Touring Cheque's 115 or so.

Either way, the savings are very real, with each voucher offering one night's pitch with electric hook-up at a set cost that can be as little as half price.

HOW ABOUT STAYING IN SPAIN FOR THE WINTER?

It's called 'overwintering' and those caravanners who've done it can't for the life of them understand why everyone else doesn't do the same. Granted, it's no use to those of us with young families or who have to work, but many first-time caravanners belong to what marketing types love to refer to as the 'silver' market, 50- or 60-somethings in retirement or semi-retirement with a nice little nest egg to maintain them in comfort.

Many such empty-nesters (there's another pigeon-hole for them), no longer needing a multi-bedroomed house, trade down to a smaller property and use some of the funds from downsizing to buy a caravan. This is perfectly understandable, given that they're ideally placed to take the fullest advantage of the freedom to get up and go that is one of the main attractions of caravanning in the first place.

In recent years, there's been a growing trend for British caravanners to pack up and head to the south of Spain (or Portugal) for the entire winter. A lot of sites that would normally close for the off-season keep their gates open to accommodate the migrating Brits, desperate to escape the gunmetal grey, damp misery of a northern European winter.

The Camping and Caravanning Club organizes winter rallies in Iberia every year, giving members the chance to travel and stay with friends and compatriots. Other caravanners are perfectly happy to do it independently, maybe arranging to meet friends en route or at the final destination.

Assuming your lifestyle allows you to go overwintering, the benefits are clear:

▶ You can virtually banish winter. Even in January, the south of Spain and Portugal are temperate enough to make a coat an optional extra.

▶ Site fees are cheap.

▶ You can appreciate all that your chosen area has to offer at a more relaxed pace, devoid of hordes of tourists.

▶ The sky-high gas and electricity bills you would normally have to suffer back home are all but eliminated.

▶ Yes, you'll still have to go food shopping; but shop wisely and your bills will be lower – fresh produce from local markets, beer and wine are all markedly cheaper than in the UK.

▶ You needn't miss out on spending Christmas with the family. Seasoned overwinterers take advantage of cheap flights to fly back to Blighty for the festive season and then (smugly) back to their winter base on the Algarve. It's also an opportunity to restock on supplies of 'essentials' that are hard to find overseas; things such as baked beans, brown sauce, mushy peas – or whatever quirky British goodies usually take your fancy. If you've no intention of making a flying visit back home, you simply need to take account of this when you leave – the generous payload of a caravan will allow you to take an awful lot of mushy peas ...

There are other considerations, though:

▶ You'll be leaving your home unattended for a very long time, with the obvious security considerations that brings. You must speak to your insurers to make sure your cover is watertight.

- Arrange for a friend, neighbour or family member to make regular visits to the house to clear mail and free newspapers away from the doormat and to check that all is generally well. Ideally, someone would be able to go in morning and evening to open and close curtains.

- Don't be caught out by unexpected bills. If you don't already do so, you can set up direct debits for the utilities – electricity, gas, water, telephone – and ask whoever's clearing your mail to forward anything that looks remotely like a bill. The caravan site owners will happily accept incoming mail for you.

- If you've not already signed up for internet banking, you should seriously consider doing so. You'll be able to keep a constant eye on your accounts wherever in the world you happen to be, and can move funds around at the click of a button.

- You will be subjecting your caravan to a period of prolonged use. That's absolutely not a problem as long as the vehicle is in tip-top condition. Have it serviced before you go and take some spare parts with you: water pump, bulbs, fuses.

- Much the same can be said about your car. As well as making sure it's mechanically sound, check when the insurance, road tax and, if applicable, the MOT are due to expire. If any coincide with the period when you'll be away, make arrangements to have them renewed beforehand.

- Don't make being locked out of either the car or caravan a bigger issue than it ought to be – take spare keys for both with you. Together with your passports, these can be left in the caravan site office's safety deposit box.

- An awning really is a prerequisite for overwintering. As we've seen, a full-size awning doubles the amount of living space at your disposal – and because we're talking of a stay running into months rather than weeks, you'll need that space to ward off any feelings that you're getting in each other's way.

Ireland

Towing speed limit

▶ 80 kph (50 mph) on single-carriageway roads outside built-up areas and motorways.

Be aware ...

▶ You can drive fully or partly on the hard shoulder – common on single-carriageway main roads – to allow following traffic to pass.

Ireland is a fantastic touring destination in its own right, but a major attraction for caravanners looking to dip their toes in the waters of a first foreign holiday is the lack of a language barrier – not to mention the fact that the Irish are the only other Europeans besides the British who drive on the left.

The Irish Caravan and Camping Council has been highly proactive in recent years, working with site owners to improve standards and promote the idea of a touring holiday to caravanners from all over Europe – but especially from the neighbouring UK.

As a result, the quality of the best Irish sites is second to none. Whether you need a base from which to explore Dublin and the Wicklow Mountains, the wild Donegal coast, the almost-too-good-to-be-true Ring of Kerry, the remote Galtee Mountains of Tipperary, the charming city of Galway or dozens of other highlights on offer on this very special island, you'll be able to stay at an excellent site. And all accompanied by the warm welcome that the Irish really do excel at – it's not some tourist board-originated myth.

Northern Ireland is, of course, part of the UK, but it shares much of the charm of its next-door neighbour. The Mountains of Mourne in County Down are among the greatest scenic gifts given to the UK – achingly beautiful, and brilliantly accessible by car, on foot or on a bike. The spectacular Antrim coast should be a must-see for anyone, and Belfast has emerged as one of the UK's most 'happening' cities, with a fantastically redeveloped waterfront and a great range of bars and restaurants in the centre.

Again, there are fine sites to stay at, including one operated by the Camping and Caravanning Club near Downpatrick – the first site outside Britain to join either of the big clubs' own networks.

Ferries sail from a number of west-coast British ports to both Northern Ireland and the Republic. The most popular options include Stranraer in south-west Scotland to Larne, just outside Belfast; and from Holyhead on the isle of Anglesey to either Dublin or nearby Dun Laoghaire.

My advice would be to choose Dun Laoghaire over Dublin if you can as the former is much more easily accessed via the impressive ring-road motorway, while you have to take your chances with the dreadful Dublin traffic if you go for the latter, which can be a problem if you have a ferry to catch.

Remember this

Dublin now benefits from a fantastic tram system, the LUAS, which is great fun to ride on and offers speedy, frequent access to the heart of the city. Better still, one of the stations is just up the road from Camac Valley, an excellent caravan site on Dublin's southern outskirts.

The Netherlands

Towing speed limit

▶ 80 kph (50 mph) on all roads and motorways.

Mandatory equipment

▶ Warning triangle.

Be aware ...

▶ You must give way to cyclists at all times.

You certainly won't be out of place touring the Netherlands in a caravan. The Dutch are the keenest caravanners in Europe and, as you would expect, there's an infrastructure to match, with hundreds of well-specified sites spread out across a country that is, away from the bigger towns and cities, very pretty. The Dutch Rhineland in particular offers a wealth of fantastic driving, cycling and walking opportunities.

It's easy to get to the Netherlands from the UK: you can sail directly to the Hook of Holland from the Essex port of Harwich or from Hull to Rotterdam. It's also no great inconvenience to land in Calais or Zeebrugge and drive north through Belgium.

There's an extensive motorway network that can speed you on your way to every part of the country – but do try to avoid using the motorways anywhere near Amsterdam or Rotterdam at peak hours, when the tailbacks can be horrendous. The rest of the roads in the Netherlands are delightful to tour on; generally speaking, they're beautifully surfaced and very well-maintained.

By all means take your Dutch phrase book with you – it's good to try mastering a few essentials, after all – but there's a very strong chance that nearly everyone you'll meet will be able to speak English at least as well as you. The Dutch are a nation of multilinguists, with English being the most widespread second language.

The Dutch are also a nation of cyclists, so do remember to pack your bikes in the caravan so you can take advantage of the spectacularly good network of dedicated cycle routes and lanes.

Belgium

Towing speed limit

- ▶ 90 kph (55 mph) on single-carriageway and dual-carriageway roads outside built-up areas.

- ▶ 120 kph (74 mph) on motorways.

Mandatory equipment

- ▶ Warning triangle, hi-viz vest for driver.

Be aware …

▶ Always give way to traffic approaching from the right, unless a sign tells you otherwise.

Belgium is overlooked by most British holidaymakers – which is a shame, because it's a far more interesting little country than it often gets credit for.

Many of its towns are very pretty (and usually spotless), with Bruges arguably being one of the finest examples of all. The hilly Ardennes, the Meuse valley and Flanders are all worth making a detour for.

In the case of the last-named, there are many poignant reminders of the cataclysmic events of the First World War, with military cemeteries, reconstructed trench formations and museums packed with artefacts and battlefield detritus.

There's no better base from which to explore Flanders than Ypres, the centre of which has been quite stunningly rebuilt to the glory it enjoyed before being reduced to a pile of rubble during the great conflict. There's a very good municipal caravan site on the edge of town.

Don't worry if you're driving around looking for Ypres but end up in a town called Ieper. They're one and the same; a perfect illustration of the confusion that lies in wait with the signposting in Belgium, which will be in either French or Flemish, depending on where you are. It's also a perfect illustration of why a visit to Belgium is an awful lot easier if you have a good map always to hand!

Germany

Towing speed limit

▶ 80 kph (49 mph) on single-carriageway roads outside built-up areas.

▶ No limit on motorways and dual carriageways, but 130 kph (80 mph) is recommended.

Recommended equipment

▶ Warning triangle, first-aid kit.

Be aware …

▶ There's a minimum speed limit of 60 kph (37 mph) on motorways. Be prepared for very fast-moving traffic in the outer lane(s).

▶ Use dipped headlights in tunnels.

If you actually enjoy driving – whether you have a caravan in tow or not – you will love Germany. Its road system is, not to put too fine a point on it, fantastic. It's rare to encounter any road without a surface that would be a credit to a race track and, in marked contrast to France and Spain, its enormous network of motorways is entirely free to use.

Similarly, the best German caravan sites are among some of the finest you'll encounter anywhere, with superb facilities and a peerless standard of presentation and cleanliness. The main tourist areas, such as the Black Forest (highly recommended), are well catered for; and riverside caravan sites are something of a speciality in Germany. In the country that boasts the Elbe, the Mosel and, of course, the Rhine, there's plenty of opportunity to find an idyllic pitch.

As you travel around, you're bound to notice how most of the towns and cities always look as though they've just had a good spring clean. They haven't; they always look like that.

In a similar vein, regular users of Britain's motorway service stations will weep when they see the German equivalents, which are almost a pleasure to visit. Caravanners are welcome to stay for up to 24 hours at these services, some of which have shower cubicles, while others have bakeries where you can start the day with fresh, warm bread.

Focus points

The main points to remember from this chapter are:

* Continental Europe is, if anything, even better-disposed towards caravanning than the UK. An overseas touring holiday is always exciting and I recommend you give it a go.

* Don't leave these shores without taking out comprehensive European breakdown and recovery cover for both car and caravan.

* Long-haul ferry crossings are expensive, but they do cut out a huge amount of driving.

* Calais is, however, a recommended port. It's quick and easy to get out of, thanks to a superb road network that soon has you on your way to your destination.

* France is a joy to tour in. Away from the bigger towns and cities, the roads are far emptier than most of us in the UK are used to.

* Filling stations can be thin on the ground in some areas of France. Fill up when you get the chance.

* Normandy is the perfect choice for a first overseas caravanning holiday. It's easy to get to, it's a fantastic region and there are plenty of cracking caravan sites.

* Spain's beautiful Costa Verde is served by Bilbao and Santander ferry ports – another way to experience a continental holiday with minimal towing.

* Many sites in the south of Spain and Portugal are geared up to accommodating the growing number of British caravanners who spend the entire winter there.

* Ireland offers a foreign holiday devoid of any concerns about driving on the 'wrong' side of the road or of mastering another language – and it has some exceptional caravan sites.

Conclusion

Make the relationship with your caravan a happy one

If you've made up your mind that you're going to take the plunge and buy that first caravan, then good for you – not many people do so and regret it. Quite the opposite, in fact: you may be about to find that caravanning will be an important part of your life.

It will be a hugely enjoyable part of your life, too, if you bear in mind these few crucial points.

▶ Be safe on the road, above all else. Whether you take my advice and test the water with a cheap and cheerful caravan or go all out and buy a brand-new one, you'll still be taking to the roads with a vehicle that needs to be safe for that purpose. If your caravan isn't new, have it checked over at a reputable caravan workshop to make sure the brakes work, that the tyres are in good condition, and that all the moving parts move as they should.

▶ Remember, towing a caravan is easy – but your skill and your confidence will be boosted enormously by taking a caravan manoeuvring course. However, if you plan to bring a caravan home this very afternoon, just one crucial reminder: keep your speed in check when descending hills, especially long, exposed motorway declines.

▶ Don't buy a caravan on your own (unless that's how you'll be using it, of course). I refer you back to Chapter 3, which stresses how crucial it is to make sure you get a caravan with a layout that suits you and your family down to the ground. Use your head, but let your heart have a say, too. If you're sitting in a caravan in the showroom, thinking: 'I'm not sure, really. There's something about this caravan but I can't quite put my finger on it …' – leave it. You'll know when you've found the one that suits you best.

- ▶ Accept that caravan theft is a problem and take all reasonable steps to make sure yours doesn't fall prey. Make sure the security devices you fit are good ones and that they comply with the conditions of your insurance policy.

- ▶ Look after your caravan and it will look after you. Keep it clean and smart, keep those cupboard doors nicely oiled, keep that carpet looking fresh, treat it to a service every year, make sure the jockey wheel and corner steadies run quietly and smoothly ... little things, but you'll get years of good service in return.

- ▶ It may seem obvious, but use your caravan. Leaving it in storage for 49 weeks of the year will be a real waste of a valuable resource that, used to its full potential, could transform your lifestyle.

Taking it further

FINDING OUT MORE – WHO TO CONTACT

Caravan Club
East Grinstead House
East Grinstead
West Sussex
RH19 1UATel: 01342 326944
www.caravanclub.co.uk

Camping and Caravanning Club
Greenfields House
Westwood Way
Coventry
CV4 8JH
Tel: 0845 130 7631
www.campingandcaravanningclub.co.uk

USEFUL WEBSITES FOR CARAVANNERS

Caravanning4U
www.caravanning4u.co.uk

Friendly, busy site with plenty of useful information on a range of topics and lots of input from caravanners, including a forum.

Caravanning Links
www.caravanninglinks.com

Something of an online directory of caravanning specialists, including reupholsterers, caravan breakers, dealers and a pretty comprehensive sitefinder facility.

ViaMichelin
www.viamichelin.com

There are many route-finding/mapping websites available – this is one of the better ones. It will even have a go at calculating how long any given journey will take you, giving you the option of inputting the type of vehicle you will be using – including a car towing a caravan.

The maps option on www.google.co.uk is also recommended.

BBC
www.bbc.co.uk

The internet is worth having for the BBC's breathtaking website alone. It's an invaluable resource for so many things. But for caravanners, the ability to key in any part of the UK and find out what the weather's going to be like locally for the next few days helps to inform last-minute getaway decisions. You can also log on to check traffic conditions before you leave.

Caravan Storage Site Owners' Association
www.cassoa.co.uk

Here, you'll find nationwide listings of all members of CaSSOA. You can click on a map of the UK to find the sites nearest to where you live.

Sold Secure Products
www.soldsecure.co.uk

This regularly updated site lists all the security products that have passed Sold Secure's stringent attack tests, with a separate section for those products specifically for use with caravans. I recommend strongly that you use only those devices that are Sold Secure-approved.

SITE GUIDES AND DIRECTORIES
Members of the two major clubs (see above) receive a variety of publications, including complete site guides to the respective club networks, plus listings for the thousands of member-only Certificated Locations and Certificated Sites (see Chapter 6 for more details).

The Caravan Club publishes *Caravan Europe*, a three-volume annual continental sites guide. Volume 1 covers France, Volume 2 covers Spain and Portugal, and Volume 3 covers virtually the rest of the continent, including the increasingly popular eastern European countries such as Slovenia, Hungary and the Czech Republic. These guides – discounted for club members – are excellent, full of advice and information and updated every year to include members' own comments on sites they've stayed at. You can buy these volumes separately.

Every two years, the Camping and Caravanning Club publishes *The Big Sites Book*, which is pretty aptly named. It's a huge tome that includes thousands of sites in the UK. Its own sites are, as you'd expect, allowed the luxury of enhanced entries.

AA Lifestyle Guide: Caravan & Camping Britain (Automobile Association)

Alan Rogers Europe: Campsite Guides (Alan Rogers Guides. Volumes available for most European countries)

The above guides come highly recommended. Every site is visited by inspectors annually, ensuring that the published verdicts are reliable.

SPECIALIST CONSUMER MAGAZINES

Practical Caravan
Teddington Studios
Broom Road
Teddington
Middlesex
TW11 9BE
Tel: 020 8267 5629
www.practicalcaravan.com

Caravan Magazine
The Maltings
West Street
Bourne
Lincolnshire
PE10 9PH
Tel: 01788 392435
www.outandaboutlive.co.uk

These magazines are published monthly, and both have their pros and cons, making it a matter of personal choice which you choose to read. As I've been editor of both, I'd better leave it at that … Both are now also available as digital magazines for Apple and Android devices.

Members of the two major clubs receive a monthly magazine as part of their membership package.

Glossary

A-frame – triangular section of the chassis at the front of the caravan, containing the handbrake, jockey wheel and hitch head.

bed locker – storage area under seat/bed.

breakaway cable – attaches to towbar structure when caravan is hitched up; designed to pull on caravan's brake in the event of it becoming uncoupled.

cassette toilet – self-contained toilet found in nearly every caravan. Cassette removes for easy, hygienic emptying.

corner steadies – four 'feet' that steady the caravan when pitched.

delamination – separation of a bond between two layers of the caravan floor; can be expensive to repair.

dinette – seating/eating area that converts to a bed or beds.

flat spot – irreparable deformation to a tyre, usually caused by prolonged parking in one position.

gas locker – bespoke, ventilated compartment for housing LPG cylinders.

gross train weight – maximum permissible weight of a laden vehicle and trailer.

hitch – the part of the caravan that couples up to the car's towball.

hook-up – connection to caravan site's mains electricity system.

jockey wheel – small wheel on A-frame, attached to a stanchion, which supports caravan when corner steadies are raised; also used as a means of levelling the caravan vertically.

kerbweight – the weight of a vehicle in its 'ready to use' condition. Precise definition varies between manufacturers. An increasingly common one is that set out under European Directive 95/48/EC: a car with the fuel tank 90 per cent full, a driver on board weighing 68 kg and luggage of 7 kg.

leisure battery – provides a 12-volt electricity supply when not using hook-up; different in specification from a standard car battery but similarly sized.

LPG – 'liquefied petroleum gas', which powers the caravan's gas appliances.

MIRO – 'mass in running order', i.e. the weight of the caravan when empty.

MTPLM – 'maximum technically permissible laden mass', i.e. the absolute maximum the caravan is permitted to weigh when laden.

noseweight – the weight borne by the towing vehicle's towbar; the vehicle will have a maximum noseweight limit, which must be adhered to.

payload – weight of all the items you load into the caravan.

pitch – area on a caravan site where you set up your caravan; varies hugely in size.

RCD – 'residual current device', which will cut off the mains electricity supply in the event of overloading the site supply or some other fault in the system.

reverse polarity – rare occurrence when connected to mains hook-up on continental sites, where live and neutral feeds become crossed.

snake – when the caravan becomes unstable on the move and begins to sway; easily avoided.

towbar – structure attached to the vehicle to enable a caravan or other trailer to be towed; a towball is part of this structure.

water ingress – damp.

Index

Notes